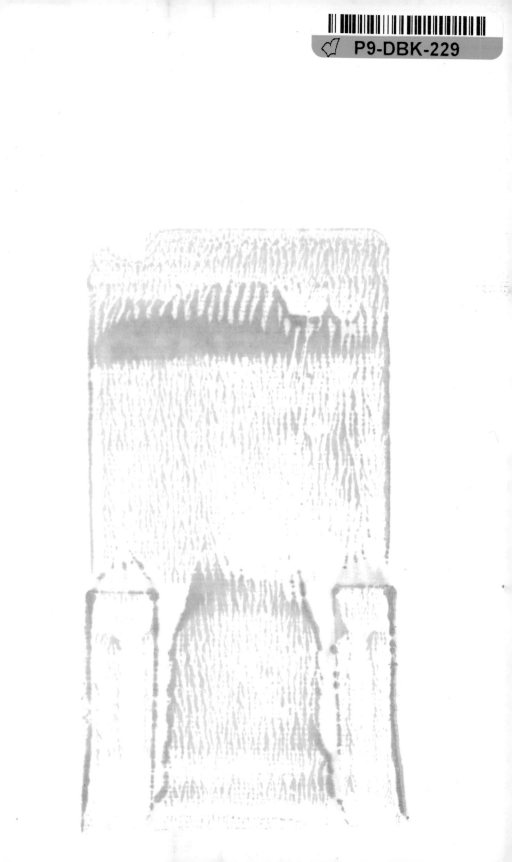

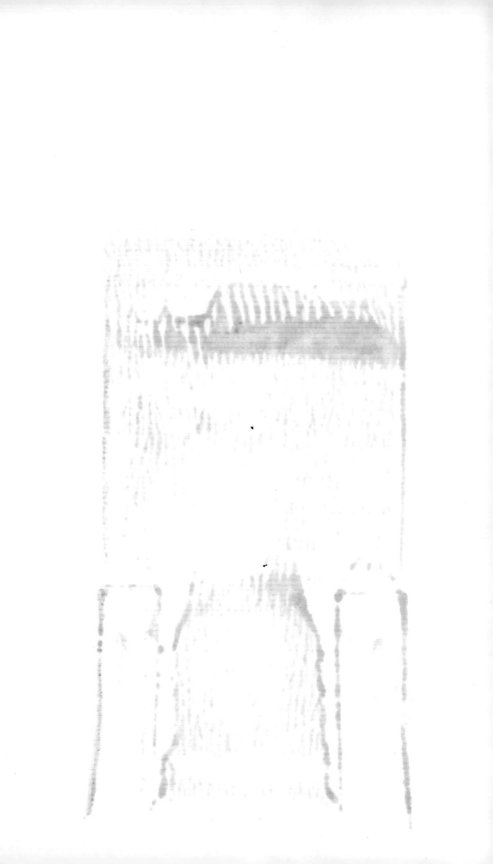

The
Erotic Elegies of
ALBIUS
TIBULLUS

WSP

WASHINGTON SQUARE PRESS

NEW YORK 1966

The
Erotic Elegies of

ALBIUS
TIBULLUS

with the poems of
Sulpicia arranged
as a sequence
called

NO
HARM
TO LOVERS

Translated by HUBERT CREEKMORE
Illustrated by EDWARD MELCARTH

85496

Library of Congress Catalog Card Number: 66–19915

Published simultaneously in the United States and Canada
by Washington Square Press

Printed in the United States of America

ACKNOWLEDGMENTS

Elegy II, 4 appeared in *The Hudson Review*, Spring, 1957. Elegies I, 9; II, 4; II, 6; and the entire group of poems by Tibullus and Sulpicia entitled *No Harm to Lovers* appeared in *Latin Poetry in Verse Translation,* edited by L. R. Lind (Houghton Mifflin, 1957). *No Harm to Lovers* also appeared in a privately printed edition in 1950 (Blue Ridge Mountain Press, Parsippany, New Jersey), and two poems from it are included in *A Little Treasury of World Poetry,* edited by Hubert Creekmore (Scribner, 1952). All of these have been revised somewhat for this volume.

Contents

INTRODUCTION
ix

BOOK I
1

BOOK II AND BOOK III
65

NO HARM TO LOVERS
103

NOTES TO THE POEMS
127

GLOSSARY
147

INTRODUCTION

I

So little is known of the Roman poet Albius Tibullus that it is impossible to place with certainty the dates of his birth and death. Yet we do know, within certain limits, when he lived. Ovid, a younger contemporary, mentions him in numerous passages, and Horace, somewhat older than Tibullus, addressed two poems to him as a friend. A lesser poet of this Augustan Age, Domitius Marsus, composed an epigram on his death:

> *You, too, Tibullus, unscrupulous Death has sent away*
> *To Elysian Fields, as Vergil's young companion;*
> *None left now weeping tender love in elegy,*
> *None singing splendid wars in heroic meter.*

From this and other bits of evidence, scholars have deduced that Tibullus died young and perhaps on the same day that Vergil died, which is known to have been September 22, 19 B.C. We infer from Horace's *Carmen* I, 33, that Tibullus was old enough to feel some drawbacks to success in love affairs:

> *Albius, don't grieve too much more at recalling*
> *Cruel Glycera, don't keep singing mournful*
> *Love-songs because one younger outshines you*
> *And her vow of true love is broken.*

It is assumed, then, that by Roman standards in this period he was not actually very young, and may have been thirty-five years old. Thus, the date of his birth may be set at about 54 B.C.

He was probably born on the country estate of his family and spent his boyhood there, as well as a part of his later life. His ancestors were aristocratic and held considerable wealth, but their land holdings had been reduced, as had those of many others, through confiscations by the government in favor of war veterans in 42, 36 or 31 B.C. Nevertheless, as Horace tells us (*Epistle,* 1, 4), he was well-to-do. The farm seems to have been located about twenty miles from Rome "in the district of Pedum"—again from Horace's *Epistle*—and Tibullus's birth there makes him one of the few great Roman poets actually born in Latium and of old native stock.

In his maturity he was handsome, refined, wealthy and famous, but probably not happy, if we are to judge from his poems. Look at the picture of him, one of the most detailed contemporary ones we have, in Horace's *Epistle:*

Albius, just and honest critic of my satires,
May I ask what you're doing now in the district of Pedum?
Composing a work which will surpass that Cassius of Parma,
Or sauntering along through healthful woods in silence,
Concerned with some deep thought befitting a wise and good
    man?
You never were a body lacking a soul: the gods
Gave you good looks and gave you wealth and the sense to
    enjoy them.
What more could a fond nurse wish for a darling foster-son,
When he is wise and can express whatever he thinks,
Is blessed with friendship, high repute, good health in abun-
    dance,
And a pleasant livelihood with never failing funds?
While involved in all your hopes and troubles, fears and anger,
Believe that every day has dawned as the last for you:
Let each hour which is not expected come as a welcome one.
Please come to see me, fat and sleek, my hide well-pampered,
And you'll want to laugh at this pig from the herd of Epicurus.

His father is thought to have died so early in Tibullus's childhood that the poet retained no definite recollections of him; but his mother and his sister lived on after the poet's death. No doubt he was sent to Rome (where he must have had a town house in later years) to be educated, and while there he became attached to the literary circle of a distinguished warrior, orator and patron of the arts.

M. Valerius Messalla Corvinus (64 B.C.–8 A.D.) was perhaps the most serious rival, as a patron in the Augustan Age, of the famous Maecenas. Though his circle included far fewer big names (Tibullus and Ovid being the only ones important today, as against Horace, Propertius, Vergil and others associated with Maecenas), it was more distinguished in character in that it was not only "unconventional, refined, delightful," but it was surprisingly unofficial and unconcerned with national affairs. To Tibullus, whose principal interests and themes were bucolic, amatory and pacifist rather than patriotic, the circle of Messalla and the relation with him—a patrician, a friend and a patron—were ideal. Such an environment was particularly suited to the writing of elegies instead of political eulogies.

II

The elegy was descended from ancient Greek poems by Archilochus and Callinus, along with the example in the *Iliad* (XXIV, 725–775), which is made up of the three laments of Andromache, Hecuba and Helen for the dead Hector. And today an elegy is generally considered a poem of lament, as we know it in Gray's "Elegy in a Country Churchyard" and Shelley's "Adonais," but the poetic form of elegy has not always been so limited in content.

By strict definition, a Greek or Roman elegy is a poem in couplets formed of a dactylic hexameter line followed by a pentameter line. It was defined, not by content or mood, but by metrics, and up to about the Second Century B.C. it treated quite varied subject matter. One genre of poetry, however, which has its own particular name, was written in elegiac couplets—epigram. Epigrams often consisted of only one couplet (the one by Domitius Marsus quoted above has two couplets), so that some distinction had to be maintained between the brief epigram or inscription and the more extended and developed elegy, though both were elegiac in meter.

The epigram, it should be noted, is not always brief and not necessarily witty, as we might suppose. In fact, many of them, having been composed as inscriptions for tombs and monuments (which is what the word means), were really laments. Many others (see the thousands in the *Greek Anthology*) are concerned with love. Thus, given the general tonal association and the actual metrical identity, it should not be surprising to find epigrams embedded in many elegies (in Tibullus, note I, 3; I, 9; his III, 20, may be considered a separate epigram).

The classics scholar Arthur Leslie Wheeler has pointed out that during the six centuries of development of the elegy, the early Greeks wrote elegies dealing with snakes, plants and travel, among other things, and that it was only in the Fourth and Third Centuries B.C. that love began to assume a considerable interest for elegists.* Before that time intimate love had been treated in epigrams and lyrics.

By the Third Century B.C., when Alexandria was the literary capital of Greece, the elegy was moving toward a greater concern with the personal sentiment of love, though not yet giving in to a personal expression of its emotion, as the remains of the works of the leading poets, Philetas and Callimachus, indicate. In the First Century B.C., the "last of the Alexandrians," Parthenius, came to the new literary capital, Rome, where he knew Gallus and Vergil and other Roman poets; and in a sense Parthenius brought with him the seeds of the "new" elegy, the intimate expression of personal love, which was to become one of the glories of Latin literature.

* Arthur Leslie Wheeler, *Catullus and the Traditions of Ancient Poetry* (Berkeley and Los Angeles: University of California Press, 1934), p. 156.

These seeds from the Alexandrian elegists found fertile ground in Catullus, though, of course, Roman writers would have known the Alexandrian poems before Parthenius's arrival. The poet's personal love, as I have said, usually found expression in lyrics or epigrams, while the elegy, when it treated of love, usually did so in a generalized manner. Callimachus, however, had been moving toward, and so was instrumental in, what Catullus at length produced—the subjective-erotic elegy. It is probably that Catullus "was not only the first Roman poet, but the first poet, Greek or Roman, to enter this field," says Professor Wheeler,* and he demonstrates how the poet has developed the materials and emotions of a two-line epigram (the famous "*Odi et amo*"—I hate and I love) into a longer poem, though still an epigram, and then into a full-blown subjective-erotic elegy. Something of this same development, although involving two poets, can be seen in the epigrams of Sulpicia herein and the brief elegies which Tibullus embroidered upon them.

So we have in Catullus the first, but not entirely smooth, accomplishment of the subjective-erotic elegy. Not entirely smooth, because the Romans were adapting into their heavy and accented language the metrical schemes of the lighter, more malleable Greek language. It is interesting to note that the hexameter line, so noble in the Greek, is considered by many to be flabby and impossible in English verse, and that we have blank verse, an iambic pentameter line, as a result of a translator's attempt to give dignity to Greek and Roman hexameters in English. We think of the mighty pentameter lines of Milton and Shakespeare and others; but to the Greeks and Romans, the pentameter was weak—"soft" and "tender." We should not be surprised, then, that the elegiac couplet, a strong hexameter with a softening pentameter, should have become the perfect verse form for expressing the intimate emotions of love.

In any case, this new form of poetry, the erotic elegy, rose

* *Op. cit.,* p. 179.

to its height within a century. We cannot say what part the poet Gallus may have played in this progress, since only a single line of his four books remains today. But, to quote again from Wheeler, "a period of about seventy-five years—from the earliest datable work of Catullus to the death of Ovid, 17 A.D.—will include the beginning, the perfection and the decline of the best Roman Elegy."*

III

Love itself hardly changes from age to age, but certain concepts of it, as expressed in the literature of each age, do vary. In Roman elegy certain conventional themes were used by the poets and should be commented upon briefly. The references given in parentheses below are to the poems of Tibullus and Sulpicia in this volume, though parallel instances may be found in other elegists of the Augustan Age.

The poets often spoke of themselves as "slaves of love" or of Venus, either in plain words (I, 1; I, 5; I, 8; II, 3; II, 4; III, 11; III, 19) or by implication (I, 2; I, 4; I, 6; I, 9; II, 6; III, 9). They conducted themselves as a slave would, bearing the nets on a hunt (I, 4; III, 9), acting as lantern-boy (I, 9), doorman (I, 1), farm-hand (II, 3) or personal attendant (I, 5), and they suffered the punishments of slaves—chains, yokes, lashings, branding and burning—figuratively, of course. Sometimes they even enjoyed the pangs of their love (II, 3; II, 6; III, 12), and even when all went smoothly, it was customary to get drunk and quarrel, fight and break up the house (I, 1; I, 10; II, 5).

The "battles of love," however, were as traditional and expected as the doors locked on the lover (I, 1; I, 2; I, 3; I, 8; II, 3; II, 4; II, 6). When the girl was "not at home," the lover usually took the garlands from round his head and hung them on the door, as a visiting card (I, 2). A doorman, a *"janitor"* (a slave chained to the doorpost), a dog, or other

* *Op. cit.,* p. 166.

guardians kept watch over the door (I, 1; I, 2; I, 6; II, 1; II, 3; II, 4).

Besides the doorkeepers, there were other obstacles to love —rivals, wealth and witchcraft. The rival was usually unknown or unnamed and was rich (I, 5; II, 4); often he was both rich and a soldier (I, 2; II, 3)—two ideas equally odious to Tibullus—or was rich and old (I, 8; I, 9). One rival (for Marathus) is named in I, 8 (Pholoë), but here even Marathus has a rival in her "hoary lover." Sulpicia too has a rival (III, 16), one from the lower classes, a status frequently implicit in the picture of the plundering soldier (II, 3). The rivals were helped at times not only by their wealth, but by bawds (I, 5; II, 6) and by witchcraft (I, 8; II, 4). The poet, however, may triumph over his rival (I, 6), may use sorcery for his own benefit (I, 2; I, 5), and may have his own accomplice in place of a bawd—for instance, the girl's mother (I, 6).

Tibullus's hatred of the rich soldier was analogous to his scorn of wealth and war (I, 1; I, 2; I, 3; I, 10; II, 3). One spawns another, and both spawn greed (I, 2; I, 3; I, 4; II, 3; II, 4). They are products of the Age of Iron, ruled by Jove (I, 3; II, 3), and bring untimely death (I, 3; I, 10) and the disruption of the happy simple life (I, 1; I, 5; I, 10; II, 1; II, 6) which was epitomized in the Golden Age of Saturn (I, 3; II, 3). This opposition of past and present was a favorite theme, and one of the earliest expressions of it, Hesiod's *Works and Days,* gave the Five Ages as ages of Gold, Silver, Bronze, Demi-gods and Iron.

One could always call upon the gods for relief, either through magic or religion, private or public rites. For these ceremonies, it was customary to have the hair loosened (in magic: II, 5; in worship: I, 1; I, 3; I, 5; I, 8) and the clothing ungirdled (in magic: I, 5; in worship: I, 3). In religious ceremonies, purity was expected, both sexual (I, 6; II, 1) and physical (I, 3; I, 8; II, 1). Purification, or lustration, was an integral part of many rituals. The whole of II, 1 concerns the lustration of the fields in the Ambarvalia; and, for personal lustration by fire, the peasants leaped across bonfires, usually three times (I, 10; II, 1; II, 5). The earthenware on which offerings were made had to be clean (I, 1), and cleanliness played a part, even in magic, in working a love charm with a torch (I, 2) or curing disease with sulphur and chanting (I, 5).

For magic, one called upon a sorceress, whose powers were conventionally described (I, 2; I, 8) in a catalogue of spells, and procured a love charm (I, 2; I, 8; II, 4). The sorceress functioned just as actively as a bawd, as mentioned above; and between the magic of the sorceress and the magic of the gods there was the fortune-reader (I, 3) for private prophecies.

Public prophecy, which tended toward religious ceremony, was of four types: fortune-telling (*sortes*), reading lots drawn from an urn (I, 3; I, 8); augury (*auspicia*), interpreting the flight, song and behavior of birds (I, 3; I, 8); haruspicy (*aruspicina*), inspecting the messages on the entrails of sacrificial victims (II, 1; II, 5); and the interpretation of the oracles in the Sibylline Books (II, 5). Only the last was restricted to the priests and for special purposes. They probably resorted to augury or haruspicy and left fortune-telling by lots to the charlatans on the streets.

In private and personal observances, the head of a household functioned as priest in the rites (II, 1; II, 2) and especially in offerings to personal gods such as the Lares (I, 1; I, 3; I, 10; II, 1), the Penates (I, 3), Priapus (I, 1; I, 4), Pales (I, 1; II, 5), Pan (II, 5), Ceres (I, 1; II, 1; II, 5), Bacchus (I, 7; II, 3) and the Guardian Spirit (Patron Spirit or Birthday Spirit) (I, 7; II, 2; III, 11; III, 12). The agricultural gods were offered first-fruits; the household gods were given holy meal, cakes, wine and honey. Milk, which had great magical properties, was poured over Pales (I, 1) and Pan (II, 5), was used by witches to lay ghosts (I, 2) and was offered with perfumes and incense at funeral rites.

Funeral customs required just the right amount of tribute

to the dead, neither too much (I, 1) nor too little (II, 4). The principal mourners, with loosened hair (I, 1; I, 3), must gather the bones and ashes of the corpse cremated on a pyre (I, 1), sprinkle them with wine and milk, mix in perfumes and store them in an urn (I, 3). Without proper tribute the dead cannot rest peacefully; and even after burial they are pleased at receiving offerings (II, 6) and anniversary wreaths (II, 4).

If magic and religion would not help, one could take consolation in the knowledge that retribution and justice would be meted out to the evil-doers through the god of vengeance (I, 8; I, 9) or through Venus, punishing those who defied her will. The perjury of a vow of love might go unpunished according to Jove (I, 4; I, 9), but not according to Venus. It was useless to resist her will (I, 8), and those who tried to do so were made to rue it. She was fierce toward all who defied her, even by making a journey (I, 4), all who mocked unhappy lovers (I, 2; I, 8), who flouted her in arrogance (II, 6), who schemed against lovers (I, 3; I, 5), or who broke their love pledges (I, 3; I, 5; I, 6; I, 9). It was even inviting her wrath to gossip about seeing a pair of lovers (I, 2; I, 6).

There was a fitness in the retribution visited on the sinners. The offending parts were punished, as in Tityos (I, 3) and the castrated priests of Ops of Ida (I, 4); or the same woe befell the offender: the daughters of Danaus must carry water for a bridal bath (I, 3); the intruding rival will be deceived in turn (I, 5); the witch who worked against the lover will also be bewitched (I, 5); the young and beautiful, when faithless, will end alone, ugly and aged (I, 6; I, 9). (Similarly, blindness was visited upon a man who looked upon forbidden rites, as in I, 6.) It was possible, however, when Venus had conferred the wrong girl upon a lover, for him to reverse the punishment onto Venus by profaning her temples (II, 4), although the satisfaction would be merely temporary.

Further comments, expanding some of the above motifs and referring to specific details not mentioned here, will be found in the appended notes; and identification of proper names, again with occasional, added information, will be found in the glossary. Though a certain amount of repetition is unavoidable in offering an introduction, notes and a glossary, it is hoped that this procedure will furnish a handy apparatus to suit the various tastes of readers. They may be ignored by many, who will feel that the poems are comprehendable and need no explanation, as is true. Other readers may find their pleasure and understanding deepened by the slight information on customs, rituals, superstitions, etc., given in the notes to each elegy. Still others may want to know more and will consult both notes and glossary.

IV

As stated before, the elegy achieved its highest formal excellence in the cultivated Augustan Age, when great attention was paid to harmony of matter and manner, rhetorical elegance, metrical and stylistic delicacy. Throughout the development of the form there had been a gradual inclination toward a subjective approach by the poets, but the subjective-erotic elegy seems to have been the particular invention of the Romans. In this characteristic Latin poem—erotic, sentimental, idyllic and ironic—Tibullus triumphed. His artistic perfection in the form (though one may grant that his spirit is typical, while that of Propertius is perhaps uncommon) and his hatred of war in a nation at the height of its military conquests give him distinction among the great writers of Augustan Rome.

Among the elegists of this period, aside from Gallus and Catullus, the outstanding ones known to us today are Propertius, Tibullus and Ovid; and of these three, Tibullus, though often acknowledged as the most perfect by writers

from the time of Quintilian* in the First Century A.D. to
scholars of the present day, is now the least known. Catullus
is famous for his savage and scatological epigrams (as is
the later Martial), somewhat less known for his lyrics, but
hardly known at all for his elegies (there are only four).
Ovid is generally known for some lyrics, better known for
his *Metamorphoses* and *Art of Love,* but scarcely known at all
for his elegies, the *Amores* (other works of his in elegiac form
are not truly subjective-erotic). Propertius and Tibullus wrote
only elegies of love, and Propertius is better known because
he has been presented by critics as a prototype of modern man
in his psychological complexity. Tibullus, who wrote in II,
1 what Gilbert Highet has called "one of the finest elegies in
the Latin language,"† is the forgotten poet of the period in
which the elegy flowered and died.

Such is his neglect in an age when Latin is rarely taught in
schools that few people, even reasonably literate ones, recognize his name. Though translations of the other major Latin
poets proliferate in this century, there are few of Tibullus.
My versions are not intended for Latin scholars, who may read
the originals with more profit and pleasure, but for the poetry-
reading public. I have taken such liberties as I felt needful to
make them as alive as they must once have been to the poet's
contemporaries. The differences of language structure make it
impossible even to suggest most of the subtleties of the original. I have not tried to render the elegiac distich of hexameter
and pentameter but have used whatever potentialities of free
verse lines I could summon to indicate the formal qualities
of the poems. I can only hope that the resulting translations

---

* *Institutes of Oratory,* 10, 1, 93: "In elegy we can challenge the
Greeks. To me Tibullus seems the most concise and polished, but some
prefer Propertius. Ovid is more wanton than either, and Gallus more
austere." (Moses Hadas, *trans.* in *A History of Rome* [New York:
Doubleday & Company, Inc., 1956].)
   † Gilbert Highet, *Poets in a Landscape* (New York: Alfred A.
Knopf, 1957), p. 168.

retain something of the spirit of Tibullus about the bare bones of substitute words.

The text used is that of the late Kirby Flower Smith's *The Elegies of Albius Tibullus* (American Book Company, 1913), and I am deeply indebted to his indispensable introduction and notes.

The
Erotic Elegies of
ALBIUS
TIBULLUS

I

DELIA
MARATHUS
MESSALLA
PHOLOË

Divitias alius fulvo sibi congerat auro
et teneat culti iugera multa soli,
quem labor adsiduus vicino terreat hoste,
Martia cui somnos classica pulsa fugent:
me mea paupertas vita traducat inerti,
dum meus adsiduo luceat igne focus.

ipse seram teneras maturo tempore vites
rusticus et facili grandia poma manu:
nec spes destituat, sed frugum semper acervos
praebeat et pleno pinguia musta lacu.

nam veneror, seu stipes habet desertus in agris
seu vetus in trivio florida serta lapis:
et quodcumque mihi pomum novus educat annus,
libatum agricolae ponitur ante deo.
flava Ceres, tibi sit nostro de rure corona
spicea quae templi pendeat ante fores:
pomosisque ruber custos ponatur in hortis
terreat ut saeva falce Priapus aves.
vos quoque, felicis quondam, nunc pauperis agri
custodes, fertis munera vestra, Lares:
tunc vitula innumeros lustrabat caesa iuvencos,
nunc agna exigui est hostia parva soli:
agna cadet vobis quam circum rustica pubes
clamet "io messes et bona vina date."

I, 1

Let others scrape together a hoard of tawny gold,
Maintain broad acres of plowed and planted land,
And daunt approaching foes with the endless toil of war
In which their sleep is routed nightly by the trumpet blasts
    of Mars:
Let my small means conduct me down a calm life-road
So long as my hearth may glow with undying fire.

Let me in proper season plant my tender grapevines
And sturdy fruit trees with skillful hands, like a peasant.
    May Hope not cheat me, but vouchsafe always
The heaps of harvest and vats abrim with rich virgin wine.

For I worship wherever a tree-trunk, lonely in the fields,
Or an ancient crossway stone is garlanded with flowers.
And whatever crops the new season brings to maturity,
First-fruits of them are set before the god of husbandry.
Ceres, flaxen-haired, let a wreath of grain-ears
Come from my fields to hang on your temple doors.
And in the fruit-filled garden let red Priapus stand guard
    To scare the crows with ferocious billhook.
You Lares, too, protectors of domains once teeming,
Now impoverished, accept your gifts.
A slaughtered heifer, then lustrated countless cattle;
Now a lamb is the humble sacrifice of my shrunken farm.
For you a lamb shall die, round which the country boys will
    shout:
        "Hurray! Give us good crops and wine!"

3

iam modo iam possim contentus vivere parvo
  nec semper longae deditus esse viae,
sed Canis aestivos ortus vitare sub umbra
  arboris ad rivos praetereuntis aquae.
nec tamen interdum pudeat tenuisse bidentem
  aut stimulo tardos increpuisse boves,
non agnamve sinu pigeat fetumve capellae
  desertum oblita matre referre domum.

at vos exiguo pecori, furesque lupique,
  parcite: de magno est praeda petenda grege.
hic ego pastoremque meum lustrare quot annis
  et placidam soleo spargere lacte Palem.
adsitis, divi, nec vos e paupere mensa
  dona nec e puris spernite fictilibus.
fictilia antiquus primum sibi fecit agrestis
  pocula, de facili composuitque luto.
non ego divitias patrum fructusque requiro
  quos tulit antiquo condita messis avo:
parva seges satis est, satis est requiescere lecto
  si licet et solito membra levare toro.
quam iuvat immites ventos audire cubantem
  et dominam tenero continuisse sinu
aut, gelidas hibernus aquas cum fuderit Auster,
  securum somnos imbre iuvante sequi!

hoc mihi contingat: sit dives iure furorem
  qui maris et tristes ferre potest pluvias.
o quantum est auri pereat potiusque smaragdi,
  quam fleat ob nostras ulla puella vias.
te bellare decet terra, Messalla, marique,
  ut domus hostiles praeferat exuvias:
me retinent vinctum formosae vincla puellae,
  et sedeo duras ianitor ante fores.
non ego laudari curo, mea Delia: tecum
  dum modo sim, quaeso segnis inersque vocer.

If only now, now, contented with my little I may live,
Never to be conscripted for remote campaigns of war,
But as the dog days loom, avoid the heat
In the shade of trees amid meandering ripply streams.
Let me not be ashamed sometimes to wield a mattock,
Or hurry sluggish oxen with a goad;
Nor irked at bringing home in my arms a stray ewe lamb
Or a newborn kid forgotten by its dam.

But all you thieves and wolves, hands off my scanty flock!
    Catch your prey from greater herds.
I must give part of mine each year to expiate my shepherds,
    Must sprinkle milk on fruitful Pales.
Stand by me, gods, don't spurn the gift from a meager hand
On clean earthenware. Of earth the primitive peasant made
Such vessels for himself and molded them of pliant clay.
I don't seek the ancestral wealth and profits
That laid-by harvests brought my grandfather long ago:
    A small field's crop is enough.
It is enough if I may rest upon my bed
And ease my limbs on my accustomed mattress.
How joyful to lie there hearing the blustering winds,
    And lock my sweetheart in tender embraces;
Or when the stormy South Wind pours cold showers,
To sleep serene and wake and doze to raindrop lullabies.

This be my fortune. Let him be rich, and rightly,
Who can endure the ocean's fury and mournful rain.
Oh, perish all gold and emeralds on the earth,
Before any girl should have to weep at my departure!
For you, Messalla, it's proper to war on land and sea
So that your porch may exhibit trophies from enemies:
For me—the bonds of a lovely girl enchain me fast,
And I sit, a slave doorkeeper, before her heartless portals.
    I don't fret for fame and applause, my Delia.
So long as I'm with you I'll ask no more than to be called
    An idler and good-for-nothing.

te spectem, suprema mihi cum venerit hora,
    te teneam moriens deficiente manu.
flebis et arsuro positum me, Delia, lecto,
    tristibus et lacrimis oscula mixta dabis.
flebis: non tua sunt duro praecordia ferro
    vincta, nec in tenero stat tibi corde silex.
illo non iuvenis poterit de funere quisquam
    lumina, non virgo, sicca referre domum.
tu manes ne laede meos, sed parce solutis
    crinibus et teneris, Delia, parce genis.

interea, dum fata sinunt, iungamus amores:
    iam veniet tenebris Mors adoperta caput:
iam subrepet iners aetas, nec amare decebit,
    dicere nec cano blanditias capite.
nunc levis est tractanda Venus, dum frangere postes
    non pudet et rixas inseruisse iuvat.
hic ego dux milesque bonus: vos, signa tubaeque,
    ite procul, cupidis vulnera ferte viris:
ferte et opes: ego composito securus acervo
    despiciam dites despiciamque famem.

When my last hour comes, let me gaze on you
And, dying, hold in my fast-failing hand your own.
You'll be weeping, Delia, as I'm set on the bier to burn,
And giving me kisses mixed with sorrowful tears.
You'll weep: your breast is not encased in hard steel,
Nor does a flint-stone lie in your tender heart.
No youth, no maid, from that funeral will go dry-eyed back
    home.
But you, Delia—don't pain my spirit; spare your unbound
    hair
From shears, spare your soft sweet cheeks from clawing nails.

Meantime, while Fate allows, let's melt our loves as one.
Soon Death comes upon us, with head in darkness shrouded;
Too soon will feeble age sneak up, and we'll be absurd
At making love and breathing gallantries with heads all white.
But now blithe passion tugs me, while smashing doors is no
    disgrace,
And tangling in wars of love is utter joy.
In them I'm a good captain and best of privates.
        Away, you trumpets and battleflags,
Confer your wounds on greedy men, and your riches with
    them!
I, safe on my harvest heap, disdain their wealth
        Just as I disdain my poverty.

I, 2

Adde merum vinoque novos compesce dolores,
    occupet ut fessi lumina victa sopor:
neu quisquam multo percussum tempora Baccho
    excitet, infelix dum requiescit amor.
nam posita est nostrae custodia saeva puellae,
    clauditur et dura ianua firma sera.

ianua difficilis domini, te verberet imber,
    te Iovis imperio fulmina missa petant.
ianua, iam pateas uni mihi, victa querellis,
    neu furtim verso cardine aperta sones.
et mala si qua tibi dixit dementia nostra,
    ignoscas: capiti sint precor illa meo.
te meminisse decet quae plurima voce peregi
    supplice, cum posti florida serta darem.

tu quoque ne timide custodes, Delia, falle;
    audendum est: fortes adiuvat ipsa Venus.
illa favet, seu quis iuvenis nova limina temptat,
    seu reserat fixo dente puella fores:
illa docet molli furtim derepere lecto,
    illa pedem nullo ponere posse sono,
illa viro coram nutus conferre loquaces
    blandaque compositis abdere verba notis.
nec docet hoc omnes, sed quos nec inertia tardat
    nec vetat obscura surgere nocte timor.

I, 2

Bring on more wine, straight wine, to drown in it these
   brand-new woes,
So sleep may seize upon my weary vanquished eyes.
And once my brain's knocked out by too much drink,
Let no one wake me while hapless love finds respite in sleep.
For a cruel guard is placed about my girl,
     Her door's shut tight, the bar shot firm.

Door of a surly master, may rain-storms flog you,
And lightning, hurled at Jove's command, strike you.
Oh door, overcome by my complaints, open now to me alone,
And when your pivot slyly turns in the socket, don't squeak.
And if my madness has called down on you a plague in any
   way,
Forgive it. Let it fall, I pray, on my own head.
You need to remember all the things I went through in sup-
   pliant voice
     While I hung flower-garlands on your posts.

And you too, Delia, fool your guardians with no fear.
You must take chances: Venus herself favors the brave.
She helps out any young man trying a strange doorway
Or a girl unlocking a bolted door with a prong.
She teaches how to creep from a soft bed stealthily,
How to set each foot down so it makes no sound,
How to speak with nods before a husband's very eyes
     And hide love-talk with made-up signs.
But she teaches this not to all, only those undelayed by sloth,
Unstayed by fear from rising in black of night.

en ego cum tenebris tota vagor anxius urbe,

*   *   *   *   *   *

nec sinit occurrat quisquam qui corpora ferro
vulneret aut rapta praemia veste petat.
quisquis amore tenetur eat tutusque sacerque
qualibet: insidias non timuisse decet.

non mihi pigra nocent hibernae frigora noctis,
non mihi, cum multa decidit imber aqua.
non labor hic laedit, reseret modo Delia postes
et vocet ad digiti me taciturna sonum.
parcite luminibus, seu vir seu femina fiat
obvia: celari vult sua furta Venus.
neu strepitu terrete pedum, neu quaerite nomen,
neu prope fulgenti lumina ferte face.
si quis et imprudens aspexerit, occulat ille
perque deos omnes se meminisse neget:
nam fuerit quicumque loquax, is sanguine natam,
is Venerem e rapido sentiet esse mari.

nec tamen huic credet coniunx tuus, ut mihi verax
pollicita est magico saga ministerio.
hanc ego de caelo ducentem sidera vidi,
fluminis haec rapidi carmine vertit iter,
haec cantu finditque solum manesque sepulcris
elicit et tepido devocat ossa rogo:
iam tenet infernas magico stridore catervas,
iam iubet aspersas lacte referre pedem.
cum libet, haec tristi depellit nubila caelo:
cum libet, aestivo convocat orbe nives.
sola tenere malas Medeae dicitur herbas,
sola feros Hecatae perdomuisse canes.
haec mihi composuit cantus, quis fallere posses:
ter cane, ter dictis despue carminibus.

See, I roam tormented all through the city in darkness,
    [And Venus keeps me safe from harm]*
And lets me meet no one who with a sword
Would stab my body or grab my cloak for plunder.
Whoever is filled with love goes, sacrosanct and safe,
Anywhere at will; he should not fear for ambush.

I feel no pain from numbing cold on winter nights,
No ache from rain downpouring in a flood.
Those hardships do not hurt if Delia but unlock the door
And mutely summon me by a finger-snap.
Don't use your eyes, if man you be, or woman, meeting us:
Venus wants her intrigues kept in hiding.
Don't scare us with clattering steps or ask our names
Or hold your flaming torches near our faces.
Should anyone have looked on us inadvertently,
    He'd better keep it secret
And swear by all the gods that he recalls it not:
For anyone who tattles will feel how Venus wields
    Her birthright of blood and furious seas.

But that husband of yours would never believe him anyway;
The trusty witch assured me this by magic means.
I've seen her draw the stars down from the sky,
With spells she reverses the course of rapid rivers.
With incantations she cracks the ground, conjures ghosts from
    tombs,
And lures the skeletons from their still warm pyres.
With magic shrilling she restrains the troops of the dead,
Then with sprinkled milk bids them withdraw.
At will she drives from gloomy skies the clouds
    Or summons snow from summer's vault.
She alone, they say, has mastered Medea's baleful herbs,
Alone has tamed the savage dogs of Hecate.

   * Conjectural lines for hiatus in Latin text.

ille nihil poterit de nobis credere cuiquam,
    non sibi, si in molli viderit ipse toro.
tu tamen abstineas aliis: nam cetera cernet
    omnia: de me uno sentiet ille nihil.

quid credam? nempe haec eadem se dixit amores
    cantibus aut herbis solvere posse meos,
et me lustravit taedis, et nocte serena
    concidit ad magicos hostia pulla deos.
non ego totus abesset amor, sed mutuus esset,
    orabam, nec te posse carere velim.

ferreus ille fuit qui, te cum posset habere,
    maluerit praedas stultus et arma sequi.
ille licet Cilicum victas agat ante catervas,
    ponat et in capto Martia castra solo,
totus et argento contextus, totus et auro,
    insideat celeri conspiciendus equo,
ipse boves mea si tecum modo Delia possim
    iungere et in solito pascere monte pecus,
et te dum liceat teneris retinere lacertis,
    mollis et inculta sit mihi somnus humo.
quid Tyrio recubare toro sine amore secundo
    prodest, cum fletu nox vigilanda venit?
nam neque tunc plumae nec stragula picta soporem
    nec sonitus placidae ducere posset aquae.

For me she fashioned a charm to help you to deceive:
Three times chant it, spit three times when the spell is said,
Then no one can make that man believe a thing about us,
Not even if he himself should see us on his feather bed.
However, you must keep away from other men,
For he'll notice all the rest. Only in me
    Will he see nothing wrong.

"Why should I trust her?" She certainly said herself she could
    loose
My love-ties by charms or simples, and she worked a torch
    lustration on me;
And in the moonlit night a black victim died
    For the powers of black magic.
But I was asking not that my love should fade
But that it be returned, for I'd not want
    To be able to do without you.

That man was made of iron who, when he could have
    had you,
Chose, big fool, to go after war and plunder.
Let him drive defeated Cilician troops before him
And pitch his martial camp on captured land.
All wound in silver stuffs, all bound in gold, focus of
    every eye,
    Let him bestride his swift horse.
If only I, with you beside me, Delia,
Can yoke my oxen and graze my herds on the same old hill,
    And clasp you close in my youthful arms,
I'll sink into sweet sleep on even the roughest ground.
What good is lying upon a Tyrian purple couch
Without love's favor, with night bringing only a vigil
    of tears?
For then no downy pillows, embroidered coverlets
Nor sounds of lulling water can induce sleep.

num Veneris magnae violavi numina verbo,
et mea nunc poenas impia lingua luit?
num feror incestus sedes adiisse deorum
sertaque de sanctis deripuisse focis?
non ego, si merui, dubitem procumbere templis
et dare sacratis oscula liminibus,
non ego tellurem genibus perrepere supplex
et miserum sancto tundere poste caput.

at tu qui laetus rides mala nostra, caveto
mox tibi: non uni saeviet usque deus.
vidi ego qui iuvenum miseros lusisset amores
post Veneris vinclis subdere colla senem
et sibi blanditias tremula componere voce
et manibus canas fingere velle comas:
stare nec ante fores puduit caraeve puellae
ancillam medio detinuisse foro.
hunc puer, hunc iuvenis turba circumterit arta,
despuit in molles et sibi quisque sinus.

at mihi parce, Venus: semper tibi dedita servit
mens mea: quid messes uris acerba tuas?

Have I in any speech profaned the will of mighty Venus,
That now my wicked tongue must pay the penalties?
Can anyone say I sinfully rushed into the gods' temples
And stole their garlands from the holy altars?
If I deserve it, I'll not flinch at falling before the temple
And covering its sacred threshold with kisses,
Nor at crawling across the ground on suppliant knees and
    beating
        My wretched head against the holy pillars.

But you there, who are gleeful and laugh at my woes,
        Just watch out soon now for yourself;
Cupid won't plague forever one lone being.
I've seen the man who mocked the pitiful loves of youth
At length when old give up his neck to Venus's yoke
And rehearse to himself soft wooings in a quavering voice
And with his fingers try to arrange his thin gray hair.
He was not ashamed to haunt his loved one's door
        Or waylay her maid in the midst of the forum.
Some youths and boys in a churning throng swarmed
    round him
And each in self-defense into his own soft bosom spat.

        Then spare me, Venus.
My heart and soul, devoted, have always served you:
Why in fury burn the harvest that's your own?

I, 3

Ibitis Aegaeas sine me, Messalla, per undas,
    o utinam memores ipse cohorsque mei:
me tenet ignotis aegrum Phaeacia terris:
    abstineas avidas, Mors precor atra, manus,
abstineas, Mors atra, precor: non hic mihi mater
    quae legat in maestos ossa perusta sinus,
non soror, Assyrios cineri quae dedat odores
    et fleat effusis ante sepulcra comis,
Delia non usquam quae, me cum mitteret urbe,
    dicitur ante omnes consuluisse deos.

illa sacras pueri sortes ter sustulit: illi
    rettulit e trinis omina certa puer.
cuncta dabant reditus: tamen est deterrita numquam,
    quin fleret nostras, respiceretque vias.
ipse ego solator, cum iam mandata dedissem,
    quaerebam tardas anxius usque moras;
aut ego sum causatus, aves dant omina dira,
    Saturni sacram me tenuisse diem.
o quotiens ingressus iter mihi tristia dixi
    offensum in porta signa dedisse pedem!
audeat invito ne quis discedere Amore,
    aut sciat egressum se prohibente deo.

quid tua nunc Isis mihi, Delia, quid mihi prosunt
    illa tua totiens aera repulsa manu,
quidve, pie dum sacra colis, pureque lavari

I, 3

You'll go on without me, Messalla, across the Aegean waves—
  Oh, think of me, you and all your staff!
Corcyra confines me, sick, in a foreign land.
Hold off your greedy hands, dark Death, I beg you,
  Sable Death, pray keep them away:
I have no mother here to gather, in mourning weeds, my
  charred bones,
No sister to bestrew my ashes with Assyrian perfumes
And weep in dishevelled tresses at my tomb.
      Nowhere a Delia who, it's said,
Consulted all the gods before she let me leave the city.

Three times she drew a sacred lot from the boy;
And the boy gleaned from the three that all was well.
      They all predicted my return.
Yet she was never dissuaded from tears and looking on
  my trip
With deep alarm. And I myself, who consoled her,
Even after I'd said goodbye always kept searching uneasily
For hindrances and delays, and found pretexts in vatic birds
Or ominous signs, or Saturn's holy day deterred me.
Oh how often, starting my journey, I claimed that my feet,
By stumbling at the door, gave woeful warnings!
Let no one dare, against Love's will, to go away
Or he'll soon learn a god forbade his leaving.

What help to me now is your Isis, Delia, what good to me
Those brazen sistra your hands so often shook,
      What good your washing yourself so clean

17

te (memini) et puro secubuisse toro?
nunc, dea, nunc succurre mihi (nam posse mederi
    picta docet templis multa tabella tuis),
ut mea votivas persolvens Delia voces
    ante sacras lino tecta fores sedeat
bisque die resoluta comas tibi dicere laudes
    insignis turba debeat in Pharia,
at mihi contingat patrios celebrare Penates
    reddereque antiquo menstrua tura Lari.

quam bene Saturno vivebant rege, prius quam
    tellus in longas est patefacta vias!
nondum caeruleas pinus contempserat undas,
    effusum ventis praebueratque sinum,
nec vagus ignotis repetens compendia terris
    presserat externa navita merce ratem.
illo non validus subiit iuga tempore taurus,
    non domito frenos ore momordit equus,
non domus ulla fores habuit, non fixus in agris
    qui regeret certis finibus arva lapis.
ipsae mella dabant quercus, ultroque ferebant
    obvia securis ubera lactis oves.
non acies, non ira fuit, non bella, nec ensem
    immiti saevus duxerat arte faber.
nunc Iove sub domino caedes et vulnera semper,
    nunc mare, nunc leti mille repente viae.

parce, pater timidum non me periuria terrent,
    non dicta in sanctos impia verba deos.
quod si fatales iam nunc explevimus annos,
    fac lapis inscriptis stet super ossa notis:

When dutifully you kept her rites,
And, well I recall, your sleeping alone in a chaste bed?
  Now, goddess, help me now,
(For your healing power is shown by many a painted board
  in your temples)
So that my Delia, giving thanks in promised prayers,
May sit at your holy portals wrapped in linen
And twice a day devote herself, with loosened hair
Notable in the throng of Pharian priests, to chanting
  your psalms.
And may I live to honor my fathers' Penates
And offer incense each month to my ancient household god.

How well man used to live with Saturn as king,
Before the earth was laid open for faraway campaigns!
The pine tree had not yet shown contempt for sky-blue waves
    And yielded its spanking sails to the winds.
Nor had the roving sailor, questing for gain in unknown lands,
    Laden his galley with foreign wares.
In those days the powerful bull had not bowed to the yoke
    Nor the horse champed the bit in a docile mouth,
No house had doors to lock, no stones, set in the fields,
    Marked fixed limits to the farms.
Of their own accord, oak trees dripped honey, and ewes,
Voluntarily coming forward, gave free-flowing milk.
No armies, no rage to kill, no war existed;
Nor had the cruel smith with brutal skill yet forged a sword.
But now in the reign of Jove, slaughter and wounds are
    ever-present,
Untimely Death comes now by sea, by a thousand other ways.

  Save me, Father above.
No false oaths, no blasphemies against the holy gods
Cause me to tremble thus in fear. But if I've now fulfilled
My allotted time, see that above my bones a stone is set.
  Carved with this epitaph:

HIC IACET IMMITI CONSVMPTVS MORTE TIBVLLVS,
MESSALLAM TERRA DVM SEQVITVRQVE MARI.

sed me, quod facilis tenero sum semper Amori,
    ipsa Venus campos ducet in Elysios.
hic choreae cantusque vigent, passimque vagantes
    dulce sonant tenui gutture carmen aves,
fert casiam non culta seges, totosque per agros
    floret odoratis terra benigna rosis:
ac iuvenum series teneris immixta puellis
    ludit, et adsidue proelia miscet Amor.
illic est cuicumque rapax Mors venit amanti,
    et gerit insigni myrtea serta coma.

at scelerata iacet sedes in nocte profunda
    abdita, quam circum flumina nigra sonant:
Tisiphoneque impexa feros pro crinibus angues
    saevit, et huc illuc impia turba fugit:
tunc niger in porta serpentum Cerberus ore
    stridet, et aeratas excubat ante fores.
illic Iunonem temptare Ixionis ausi
    versantur celeri noxia membra rota,
porrectusque novem Tityos per iugera terrae
    adsiduas atro viscere pascit aves.
Tantalus est illic, et circum stagna: sed acrem
    iam iam poturi deserit unda sitim:
et Danai proles, Veneris quod numina laesit,
    in cava Lethaeas dolia portat aquas.
illic sit quicumque meos violavit amores,
    optavit lentas et mihi militias.

HERE LIES TIBULLUS, FELLED BY CRUEL DEATH
WHILE FOLLOWING MESSALLA ACROSS THE SEAS AND EARTH.

But since I always was susceptible to gentle Love,
Venus herself shall lead me to the Elysian Fields.
There dancing and singing flourish, and birds flitting here
    and there
        Pour out sweet tunes from slender throats.
The fields, untilled, bear cinnamon, and all through the land
The gracious earth is blooming fragrant roses.
And teams of youths, joined with gentle girls, play games,
And Love continually embroils them in battle.
There dwell all lovers whom greedy Death surprised
And, as a signal honor, wear myrtle wreaths around their hair.

But the abode of wicked men lies plunged
In the farthest deeps of night with black rivers roaring
    round it:
And Tisiphone, dishevelled, with savage snakes as tresses,
Rages there, and sinful hordes flee pell-mell before her.
While at the gates black Cerberus with serpents' tongues
Gives hisses and stands his guard before the doors of bronze.
Down there the guilty limbs of Ixion, who had dared
To assault Juno, are whirled on a rapid wheel,
And Tityos, stretched across nine acres of land,
Feeds insatiable birds on his black heart and liver.
There too is Tantalus, ringed by pools: but just when he
    would drink,
The flood draws back from his burning thirst.
And Danaus' daughters, because they flouted the will
    of Venus,
Carry Lethean water in jars full of holes.
May all go there who have desecrated my love and yours,
And wished on me a war expedition long drawn out.

at tu casta precor maneas, sanctique pudoris
    adsideat custos sedula semper anus.
haec tibi fabellas referat positaque lucerna
    deducat plena stamina longa colo.
at circa gravibus pensis adfixa puella
    paulatim somno fessa remittat opus.
tunc veniam subito, nec quisquam nuntiet ante,
    sed videar caelo missus adesse tibi.
tunc mihi, qualis eris, longos turbata capillos,
    obvia nudato, Delia, curre pede.
hoc precor, hunc illum nobis Aurora nitentem
    Luciferum roseis candida portet equis.

I,4

"Sic umbrosa tibi contingant tecta, Priape,
    ne capiti soles, ne noceantque nives:
quae tua formosos cepit sollertia? certe
    non tibi barba nitet, non tibi culta coma est,
nudus et hibernae producis frigora brumae,
    nudus et aestivi tempora sicca Canis."

sic ego: tum Bacchi respondit rustica proles
    armatus curva sic mihi falce deus.

"o fuge te tenerae puerorum credere turbae:
    nam causam iusti semper amoris habent.
hic placet, angustis quod equum compescit habenis:

But pray keep chaste and true, my Delia,
And let the zealous nurse always beside you guard your
   stainless modesty.
She'll be telling you stories and when the lamp is set out,
Drawing lengthy threads from the laden distaff;
And all around you the maids, intent on the heavy stint,
Will one by one leave off their work, worn out for sleep.
Then, unexpected, may I come, with none to announce it.
   Let me seem to drop from the clouds before you.
Then, just as you are, Delia, with long hair loose and tumbled,
Run to meet me on your naked feet. I pray for this:
May radiant Aurora bring to me this yearned-for day
   On the rosy horses of gleaming Lucifer.

I,4

"If you would have a leafy roof of shade, Priapus,
So stinging sun and snow won't harm your head,
Tell me what tricks you know to capture handsome boys.
After all, your beard's not sleek, your hair's not even combed.
Stark naked you stand out through the cold of wintry storms,
And naked in the furnace of the Dog Star's droughts."

That's what I said: and Bacchus' rustic offspring,
A god armed with a curving billhook, intoned:

"Oh beware entrusting yourself to those tender gangs of boys,
For they always show good reason for being loved.
One pleases because he grips a tight rein on his horse;

hic placidam niveo pectore pellit aquam:
hic, quia fortis adest audacia, cepit: at illi
virgineus teneras stat pudor ante genas.

sed ne te capiant, primo si forte negabit,
    taedia: paulatim sub iuga colla dabit.
longa dies homini docuit parere leones,
    longa dies molli saxa peredit aqua:
annus in apricis maturat collibus uvas,
    annus agit certa lucida signa vice.

nec iurare time: Veneris periuria venti
    irrita per terras et freta summa ferunt.
gratia magna Iovi: vetuit pater ipse valere
    iurasset cupide quidquid ineptus amor:
perque suas impune sinit Dictynna sagittas
    adfirmes, crines perque Minerva suos.

at si tardus eris, errabis: transiet aetas:
    quam cito non segnis stat remeatque dies,
quam cito purpureos deperdit terra colores,
    quam cito formosas populus alba comas!
quam iacet, infirmae venere ubi fata senectae,
    qui prior Eleo est carcere missus equus!
vidi iam iuvenem, premeret cum serior aetas,
    maerentem stultos praeteriisse dies.
crudeles divi! serpens novus exuit annos:
    formae non ullam fata dedere moram.
solis aeterna est Baccho Phoeboque iuventas:
    nam decet intonsus crinis utrumque deum.

tu, puero quodcumque tuo temptare libebit,
    cedas: obsequio plurima vincit amor.
neu comes ire neges, quamvis via longa paretur
    et Canis arenti torreat arva siti,

Another because he cleaves a placid stream with
   snow-white breast.
This, because he's charged with cocky mettle, charms you;
Or that, for the virgin modesty that stands forth on soft cheeks.

"But don't, if he by chance refuse at first, let boredom take you.
By slow degrees he'll slide his neck into the yoke.
For time at length can teach a lion to yield to man,
   In time weak water eats away stone.
A year matures the grapes on sunny slopes, a year's course rolls
   The bright zodiac in its fixed orbit.

"Don't fear to pledge. By winds the perjuries of love
Are blown, null and void, across the land and farthest seas.
Many thanks to Father Jove; our lord himself decreed
Invalid whatever foolish lovers in passion's heat might swear.
Net-hung Diana will let you vow by all her arrows,
Minerva, by her very hair, and no harm done.

"But if you tarry, you will lose. Youth flies away:
   How quickly unlagging suns can set and return!
   How fast earth loses its roseate complexion!
   How soon tall poplars are bald of lovely leaves!
   How downcast, when fated feeble age draws near,
The horse that once in Elis sprang from the starting post!
I've seen young men, with ripe age pressing hard,
Lament the long-gone days they wasted stupidly.
Cruel gods! The snake, shedding his skin of years, is young.
   Fate gives beauty no reprieve.
None but Bacchus and Phoebus are young forever,
For flowing uncut hair is the mark of both these gods.

"So you, whatever your boy would like to try, give in.
   Love conquers most by fond indulgence.
Never refuse to go with him, however long a hike be planned,
And dog days scorch the fields with parching drought,

quamvis praetexens picea ferrugine caelum
    venturam admittat nimbifer Eurus aquam.
vel si caeruleas puppi volet ire per undas,
    ipse levem remo per freta pelle ratem.
nec te paeniteat duros subiisse labores
    aut opera insuetas atteruisse manus,
nec, velit insidiis altas si claudere valles,
    dum placeas, umeri retia ferre negent.
si volet arma, levi temptabis ludere dextra:
    saepe dabis nudum, vincat ut ille, latus.

tum tibi mitis erit, rapias tum cara licebit
    oscula: pugnabit, sed tamen apta dabit.
rapta dabit primo, mox offeret ipse roganti,
    post etiam collo se implicuisse velit.

heu male nunc artes miseras haec saecula tractant:
    iam tener absuevit munera velle puer.
at tua, qui Venerem docuisti vendere primus,
    quisquis es, infelix urgeat ossa lapis.

Pieridas, pueri, doctos et amate poetas,
    aurea nec superent munera Pieridas.
carmine purpurea est Nisi coma: carmina ni sint,
    ex umero Pelopis non nituisset ebur.
quem referent Musae, vivet dum robora tellus,
    dum caelum stellas, dum vehet amnis aquas.
at qui non audit Musas, qui vendit amorem,
    Idaeae currus ille sequatur Opis
et tercentenas erroribus expleat urbes
    et secet ad Phrygios vilia membra modos.
blanditiis vult esse locum Venus ipsa: querellis
    supplicibus, miseris fletibus illa favet."

Though shrouding the skies with pitchy purple gloom,
Eurus, wind of storms, whips on the coming rain.
Or if he wants to skim the azure waves in a skiff,
Take the oars yourself and row the light boat across the sound.
Don't be sorry to suffer harsh exertions,
Or scratch and blister your hands in work you've never done.
If he would block the mountain vales with snares,
Provided you please, don't let your shoulders refuse to bear
    the nets.
If he would fence, you are to feint your parries with easy hand
And often leave your side exposed, so he may win.

"Then he'll be ripe for you, he'll let you steal a sweet kiss.
He'll fight, but still let your lips cling close.
At first he'll let you snatch it, later give more for the asking,
And finally even long to twine about your neck.

"But alas, our corrupt generation traffics in evil arts.
        Today young boys expect to get a present.
You who first taught putting a price on sex,
Whoever you are, may a damned gravestone crush your bones!

"To the Pierian Maids, to gifted poets, give your love, boys.
Count no gifts of gold worth more than the Pierian Maids.
In poems the forelock of Nisus is ever purple;
Except for poems, no ivory would have gleamed on
    Pelops' shoulder.
The man of whom the Muses tell shall live
While the earth bears oaks, while rivers hold water,
        While the heavens sail the stars.
But he who is deaf to the Muses, who sells his love,
May he lurch behind the chariot of Ops of Ida
And haunt with his vagrancy three hundred cities
And, to Phrygian screeching, slash off his parts so little prized.
Venus herself wants to be the cause for love-making.
To pleading complaints, to wretched tears she gives her aid."

haec mihi, quae canerem Titio, deus edidit ore:
 sed Titium coniunx haec meminisse vetat.
pareat ille suae: vos me celebrate magistrum,
 quos male habet multa callidus arte puer.
gloria cuique sua est: me qui spernentur amantes
 consultent: cunctis ianua nostra patet.
tempus erit, cum me Veneris praecepta ferentem
 deducat iuvenum sedula turba senem.

heu heu quam Marathus lento me torquet amore!
 deficiunt artes, deficiuntque doli.
parce, puer, quaeso, ne turpis fabula fiam,
 cum mea ridebunt vana magisteria.

I, 5

Asper eram et bene discidium me ferre loquebar:
 at mihi nunc longe gloria fortis abest.
namque agor ut per plana citus sola verbere turben
 quem celer adsueta versat ab arte puer.
ure ferum et torque, libeat ne dicere quicquam
 magnificum post haec: horrida verba doma.

parce tamen, per te furtivi foedera lecti.
 per Venerem quaeso compositumque caput.
ille ego, cum tristi morbo defessa iaceres,

All this the god brought forth from his mouth for me
   to sing to Titius:
But Titius' wife says he must not recall such things.
    Let him heed his mate.
But you, whom a sly boy plagues with many wiles,
Flock now to me, the new expert in love.
To each his glory comes: mine, that lovers spurned consult me.
    Open stands my door to all.
The time shall come when zealous crowds of youths
Shall escort me, an old man glossing the precepts of Venus,
   on my way.

Oh god! How Marathus tortures me with doled-out love!
My knowledge is a failure, my guiles a failure.
Spare me, boy, I beg you, lest I become ugly town-talk,
    When people will laugh at my futile lessons!

I, 5

I was angry, said I could easily stand our breaking up;
But now my reckless heroics are far, far gone.
For like a top I'm driven, spun along the flat ground by a whip,
    By a rash Boy whirled with seasoned skill.
Burn, rack your untamed slave, till he have no taste hereafter
To bray a mighty boast. Suppress his rough remarks.

Yet spare me, I pray, by the bonds of our secret bed,
Our coupling in love, with your head pressed at my cheek!
When you lay stricken by dark disease, they'll tell you,

te dicor votis eripuisse meis:
ipseque te circum lustravi sulfure puro,
  carmine cum magico praecinuisset anus:
ipse procuravi ne possent saeva nocere
  somnia, ter sancta deveneranda mola:
ipse ego velatus filo tunicisque solutis
  vota novem Triviae nocte silente dedi.
omnia persolvi: fruitur nunc alter amore,
  et precibus felix utitur ille meis.

at mihi felicem vitam, si salva fuisses,
  fingebam demens, sed renuente deo.
rura colam, frugumque aderit mea Delia custos,
  area dum messes sole calente teret,
aut mihi servabit plenis in lintribus uvas
  pressaque veloci candida musta pede.
consuescet numerare pecus, consuescet amantis
  garrulus in dominae ludere verna sinu.
illa deo sciet agricolae pro vitibus uvam,
  pro segete spicas, pro grege ferre dapem.
illa regat cunctos, illi sint omnia curae:
  at iuvet in tota me nihil esse domo.
huc veniet Messalla meus, cui dulcia poma
  Delia selectis detrahat arboribus:
et tantum venerata virum, hunc sedula curet,
  huic paret atque epulas ipsa ministra gerat.
haec mihi fingebam, quae nunc Eurusque Notusque
  iactat odoratos vota per Armenios.

saepe ego temptavi curas depellere vino:
  at dolor in lacrimas verterat omne merum.

I was the one who snatched you back by my solemn vows;
I who circled you to purge with cleansing sulphur
After the crone had chanted magic incantations;
I myself who expiated the evil dreams
Which must be prayed away three times with gifts of
   holy meal
     So that they might be rendered harmless;
I myself, enveloped in woolen cowl and loosened tunic,
Made nine vows to Trivia in the dead of night.
All this I did for you: now another enjoys my darling—
     And he, lucky man, profits by my prayers!

Still I used to picture to myself—insane of me!—
A happy life ahead if you were cured: but the gods refused.
"I'll live in the country, and my Delia shall guard the harvest
As grain is winnowed on the threshing floor in the hot sun.
     She'll tend my grapes in the laden tubs
      Where swift feet tread the sparkling must.
She'll soon get used to counting cattle, used to bouncing
A babbling baby slave on his loving mistress' lap.
She'll know to offer the god of farmers grapes for vineyards,
Grain-spikes for fields, a solemn feast for flocks.
Let her direct all chores, the whole thing be her charge.
I'll revel in being a mere nothing around the house.
Here my friend Messalla will come, for whom
Delia will pull sweet fruit from the choicest trees
     And, honoring so great a man,
Will tend him closely, cook and serve a meal to him
     And act the maid herself."
All this I used to dream, I whose prayers the wild winds
Of East and South now scatter across perfumed
   Armenian lands.

I often tried to drive my worries away with wine,
     But anguish turned all the drinks to tears.

saepe aliam tenui: sed iam cum gaudia adirem,
    admonuit dominae deseruitque Venus.
tunc me discedens devotum femina dixit,
    et pudet et narrat scire nefanda meam.
non facit hoc verbis, facie tenerisque lacertis
    devovet et flavis nostra puella comis.
talis ad Haemonium Nereis Pelea quondam
    vecta est frenato caerula pisce Thetis.

haec nocuere mihi, quod adest huic dives amator:
    venit in exitium callida lena meum.
sanguineas edat illa dapes atque ore cruento
    tristia cum multo pocula felle bibat:
hanc volitent animae circum sua fata querentes
    semper, et e tectis strix violenta canat:
ipsa fame stimulante furens herbasque sepulcris
    quaerat et a saevis ossa relicta lupis,
currat et inguinibus nudis ululetque per urbes,
    post agat e triviis aspera turba canum.
eveniet: dat signa deus: sunt numina amanti,
    saevit et iniusta lege relicta Venus.

at tu quam primum sagae praecepta rapacis
    desere: nam donis vincitur omnis amor.
pauper erit praesto semper tibi: pauper adibit
    primus et in tenero fixus erit latere:
pauper in angusto fidus comes agmine turbae
    subicietque manus efficietque viam:
pauper ad occultos furtim deducet amicos
    vinclaque de niveo detrahet ipse pede.

I often hugged another girl, but just when I verged on bliss
Venus called to mind my sweetheart and left me sad and limp.
At that the girl, stalking out, said I was bewitched,
Filled me with shame and told that my love could work
  black magic.
But no: my girl does this not by a spell;
By a lovely face, soft arms, and flaxen hair she
  bewitches me.
Like her was Thetis, Nereid of sky-blue eyes,
Once borne on a bridled dolphin to Peleus of Thessaly.

Here's what's ruining me: because a rich suitor courts her,
    A cunning madam plots my downfall.
    May this hag gobble banquets of blood,
With gory lips gulp brimming cups of puckering gall!
May love-ghosts, wailing their murder, swirl around
  her forever,
    And a raucous screech-owl shriek on her roof!
Rabid from goading hunger, may she crop grass from graves,
And gnaw on bones that savage wolves have left,
    And reel about with her belly bare
And howl through towns, from even the crossways chased
    By savage packs of dogs.
This will come to pass: the god gives a sign.
There's divine power in favor of lovers, and Venus,
    When left for an unjust contract, is ruthless.

But you, my sweet, as soon as possible renounce
This greedy crone's instructions; for every love is vanquished
  by gifts.
    A poor man will serve you always, a poor man
Will come to you first and stand firm by your soft young side.
He'll be a faithful comrade in the jostling surge of crowds,
And push his hands between to make a passage for you.
He'll sneak you out to private stag suppers
And himself will take the sandals off your snowy feet.

heu canimus frustra, nec verbis victa patescit
    ianua, sed plena est percutienda manu.

at tu qui potior nunc es, mea fata timeto:
    versatur celeri Fors levis orbe rotae.
non frustra quidam iam nunc in limine perstat
    sedulus ac crebro prospicit ac refugit
et simulat transire domum, mox deinde recurrit
    solus et ante ipsas exscreat usque fores.
nescio quid furtivus amor parat utere quaeso,
    dum licet: in liquida nat tibi linter aqua.

I, 6

Semper, ut inducar, blandos offers mihi vultus,
    post tamen es misero tristis et asper, Amor.
quid tibi saevitiae mecum est? an gloria magna est
    insidias homini composuisse deum?

nam mihi tenduntur casses: iam Delia furtim
    nescio quem tacita callida nocte fovet.
illa quidem tam multa negat, sed credere durum est:
    sic etiam de me pernegat usque viro.
ipse miser docui quo posset ludere pacto
    custodes: heu heu nunc premor arte mea.
fingere tunc didicit causas, ut sola cubaret,

I sing, alas, in vain: not to words will her door swing open,
Conquered; it must be knocked upon by a lavish hand.

But you who're now in the saddle, beware a fate like mine.
Fickle Luck changes with each quick turn of her wheel.
Not for nothing does someone even now
Keep busy watch at her porch, and gaze and gaze and
    dart away,
Pretend to pass the house, then run straight back alone,
And hawk and spit incessantly before the very door.
I don't know what sly Love is scheming. I simply beg you,
Make the most of it while it's your turn:
        Your skiff sails calm and shimmering seas.

I, 6

Always, to lure me on, Cupid, you show an inviting face,
But later you're stern and cruel to me, poor wretch.
Why do you vent your rage on me? Is it indeed great glory
    To a god to rig up snares for a man?

For nets are spread for me; already wily Delia
Slyly snuggles warm in the silent night with—
    I don't know who it is.
She denies it so much it's hard to believe her.
Thus also to her husband she firmly denies my doings.
      And I, poor numbskull, taught her the ways
      By which she could deceive her guardians.

cardine tunc tacito vertere posse fores:
tunc sucos herbasque dedi, quis livor abiret
quem facit impresso mutua dente Venus.

at tu, fallacis coniunx incaute puellae,
   me quoque servato, peccet ut illa nihil.
neu iuvenes celebret multo sermone caveto
   neve cubet laxo pectus aperta sinu,
neu te decipiat nutu, digitoque liquorem
   ne trahat et mensae ducat in orbe notas.
exibit quam saepe, time, seu visere dicet
   sacra bonae maribus non adeunda deae.
at mihi si credas, illam sequar unus ad aras:
   tunc mihi non oculis sit timuisse meis.
saepe, velut gemmas eius signumque probarem,
   per causam memini me tetigisse manum:
saepe mero somnum peperi tibi, at ipse bibebam
   sobria supposita pocula victor aqua.

non ego te laesi prudens: ignosce fatenti;
   iussit Amor: contra quis ferat arma deos?
ille ego sum, nec me iam dicere vera pudebit,
   instabat tota cui tua nocte canis.
quid tenera tibi coniuge opus? tua si bona nescis
   servare, frustra clavis inest foribus.
te tenet, absentes alios suspirat amores
   et simulat subito condoluisse caput.
at mihi servandam credas: non saeva recuso
   verbera, detrecto non ego vincla pedum.
tum procul absitis, quisquis colit arte capillos,
   et fluit effuso cui toga laxa sinu:

Now, alas, I'm trapped by my own cleverness.
From me she learned how to feign pretexts for sleeping alone,
From me how she could open a door on noiseless pivots.
At the time I gave her lotions and herbs to banish the bruises
Caused by imprints of teeth while making love to each other.

Now look, you reckless sex-mate of this tricky girl,
See you also protect my claims, that she may do no wrong.
Be sure she doesn't visit young men and prattle away,
Or loll around with robes agape on naked breasts,
Or deceive by winks or dip her finger in wine
      And scribble signs on the table-top.
      If she goes out often, beware,
Or if she says she'd watch the rites of the Good Goddess,
      Near which no male must go.
But trust her to me, let none else squire her to the temple;
Then, with her to look at, I need fear no blinding
    for sacrilege.
Often, as if to study her jeweled rings—a mere pretext—
      I remember touching her hand.
Often I drank you to sleep on wine, though I, triumphant,
Was drinking sober cups of water instead.

I didn't injure you on purpose. Forgive me,
Since I confess: Cupid made me do it.
      And who can fight against the gods?
I'm the man—and now I'm not ashamed to tell the truth—
At whom your house-dog growled the whole night long.
      What good's a tender wife to you?
If you can't keep your fortune safe, no use to lock your doors.
She hugs you, heaves a sigh (for another lover, absent),
Then suddenly pretends a splitting headache.
      So into my keeping you ought to commit her.
I don't mind the fierce knouts of love, I don't refuse
      Its fetters on my feet.

quisquis et occurret, ne possit crimen habere,
    stet procul ante alia, stet procul ante via.

sic fieri iubet ipse deus, sic magna sacerdos
    est mihi divino vaticinata sono.
haec ubi Bellonae motu est agitata, nec acrem
    flammam, non amens verbera torta timet:
ipsa bipenne suos caedit violenta lacertos
    sanguineque effuso spargit inulta deam,
statque latus praefixa veru, stat saucia pectus,
    et canit eventus quos dea magna monet.
"parcite quam custodit Amor violare puellam,
    ne pigeat magno post didicisse malo.
attigerit, labentur opes, ut vulnere nostro
    sanguis, ut hic ventis diripiturque cinis."
et tibi nescio quas dixit, mea Delia, poenas:
    si tamen admittas, sit precor illa levis.

non ego te propter parco tibi, sed tua mater
    me movet atque iras aurea vincit anus.
haec mihi te adducit tenebris multoque timore
    coniungit nostras clam taciturna manus:
haec foribusque manet noctu me adfixa proculque
    cognoscit strepitus me veniente pedum.
vive diu mihi, dulcis anus: proprios ego tecum,
    sit modo fas, annos contribuisse velim.
te semper natamque tuam te propter amabo:
    quidquid agit, sanguis est tamen illa tuus.
sit modo casta, doce, quamvis non vitta ligatos
    impediat crines nec stola longa pedes.

Then stay far away, all you who dress your hair with chic,
Whose sweeping togas undulate in lavish folds.
And any who walks abroad, lest a curse befall you,
Keep out of sight on other lanes, or far ahead in the street.

This the Love-god himself orders to be done,
This the mighty priestess foretold to me in prophetic words:
Excited by Bellona's inspiration, delirious,
She fears not biting flames nor knotted whips.
With a two-edged ax this furious woman cuts her arms
And, numb to pain, asperges the image with spurting blood,
Stands fixed, with javelin piercing her side, with
    bosom wounded,
And chants the fate the great goddess puts in her mouth:
"Forbear from injuring the girl whom Love protects,
Lest afterward you regret being taught a lesson with great woe.
Tamper with her and your wealth shall spill and fall
As the blood from my wound, as these ashes snatched by
    the wind."
And she fixed some kind of penalty for you, dear Delia.
If you incur it nevertheless, I pray she make it mild.

Not for your own self do I spare you—your mother moves
    my heart,
        Her golden ripe age quells my anger.
She waits for me unbudging by the door at night,
From afar she knows the sound of my approaching feet,
She leads me to you in the dark, and all a-twitter,
Without a word, entwines our hands in secret privacy.
        Long may you live, my sweet old woman!
To your own span of life, if heaven only agreed,
I'd add my own. I'll always love you, and because of you,
Your daughter. No matter what she does, she's still your child.
        Just teach her to be true and pure,
Though no patrician fillet rings her bound-up hair,
        No matron's gown trails at her feet.

et mihi sint durae leges, laudare nec ullam
     possim ego quin oculos appetat illa meos:
et si quid peccasse putet, ducarque capillis
     immerito pronas proripiarque vias.
non ego te pulsare velim, sed, venerit iste
     si furor, optarim non habuisse manus.
nec saevo sis casta metu, sed mente fideli:
     mutuus absenti te mihi servet amor.

at quae fida fuit nulli, post victa senecta
     ducit inops tremula stamina torta manu
firmaque conductis adnectit licia telis
     tractaque de niveo vellere ducta putat.
hanc animo gaudente vident iuvenumque catervae
     commemorant merito tot mala ferre senem:
hanc Venus ex alto flentem sublimis Olympo
     spectat et infidis quam sit acerba monet.

haec aliis maledicta cadant: nos, Delia, amoris
     exemplum cana simus uterque coma.

I,7

Hunc cecinere diem Parcae fatalia nentes
     stamina non ulli dissoluenda deo:
hunc fore Aquitanas posset qui fundere gentes,
     quem tremeret forti milite victus Atax.

And let harsh conditions apply to me, may I not praise
Any girl without my Delia clawing at my eyes.
　　And if she thinks I've played her false,
Grab me, though innocent, by the hair and drag me
Headlong down the streets. I wouldn't want to strike you,
But if such a rage beset me, I hope I have no hands.
Keep chaste, not from cruel fear, but a faithful heart.
Let our love for each other guard you for me when I'm away.

For the woman who was true to no man, when poor and bent
Later on with age, draws out with tremulous hand the
　　twisted thread,
Ties fast the thrums to the loom and cleans the carded flocks
　　Of snowy wool to earn her wages.
Throngs of young men with joyful hearts gloat over her
And remember the old woman bears so much woe as
　　due reward.
From lofty Olympus sublime Venus gazes on her weeping
And warns false lovers how ruthless she can be.

Let those curses fall on others! Delia, let us both
Be model lovers even when our hair is white.

I,7

This day the Fates forecast in song, spinning threads
　　Of destiny no god can sunder:
This to be the day which could rout the Aquitanian tribes
And make the Aude, conquered by brave soldiers, tremble.

evenere: novos pubes Romana triumphos
    vidit et evinctos bracchia capta duces:
at te victrices lauros, Messalla, gerentem
    portabat niveis currus eburnus equis.

non sine me est tibi partus honos: Tarbella Pyrene
    testis et Oceani litora Santonici,
testis Arar Rhodanusque celer magnusque Garumna,
    Carnutis et flavi caerula lympha Liger.
an te, Cydne, canam, tacitis qui leniter undis
    caeruleus placidis per vada serpis aquis,
quantus et aetherio contingens vertice nubes
    frigidus intonsos Taurus alat Cilicas?
quid referam ut volitet crebras intacta per urbes
    alba Palaestino sancta columba Syro,
utque maris vastum prospectet turribus aequor
    prima ratem ventis credere docta Tyros,
qualis et, arentes cum findit Sirius agros,
    fertilis aestiva Nilus abundet aqua?

Nile pater, quanam possim te dicere causa
    aut quibus in terris occuluisse caput?
te propter nullos tellus tua postulat imbres,
    arida nec pluvio supplicat herba Iovi.
te canit atque suum pubes miratur Osirim
    barbara, Memphiten plangere docta bovem.
primus aratra manu sollerti fecit Osiris
    et teneram ferro sollicitavit humum,
primus inexpertae commisit semina terrae
    pomaque non notis legit ab arboribus.
hic docuit teneram palis adiungere vitem,
    hic viridem dura caedere falce comam:
illi iucundos primum matura sapores

So has it happened: Romans have seen new triumphs,
    Commanders with limbs bound up in chains.
And you, Messalla, wearing the victor's laurels,
Were carried in an ivory chariot with sleek white horses.

Not without me was your honor gained. The
    Tarbellian Pyrenees
Bear witness, the Santonian shores of Ocean, the Saone,
Swift Rhone and mighty Garonne bear witness,
And Loire, the sky-hued stream of the blond men of Chartres.
    Or should I sing of you, Cydnus,
Gliding in muted ripples, calm, glass-hued,
    Along your bed of placid waters,
And how, with summit touching the air-borne clouds,
Frosty Taurus nourishes the rough unshorn Cilicians?
Why should I tell how, through teeeming cities,
The white dove sacred to Palestinian Syria flies unharmed;
How Tyre, the first with skill to trust ships to the winds,
Looks from its towers over the vast sea-prairie;
And how, when the Dog Star cracks the scorching fields,
Fertilizing Nile overflows with water in summer's heat?

Father Nile, how can I explain the cause of this,
    Or in what lands you have hidden your head?
Because of you, your soil begs for no showers,
No dry grasses implore Rain-bringing Jove.
People praise and revere you as their own Osiris,
Barbaric people taught to bewail the Memphian
    bullock, Apis.
Osiris first made plows with his inventive hands.
And stirred soft loam with an iron share;
He first entrusted seeds to unproven earth,
And gathered fruit from trees unknown before.
He taught man how to tie young vineshoots to the stakes.
And prune the greening leaves with a stern knife;

expressa incultis uva dedit pedibus.
ille liquor docuit voces inflectere cantu,
    movit et ad certos nescia membra modos:
Bacchus et agricolae magno confecta labore
    pectora tristitiae dissoluenda dedit:
Bacchus et adflictis requiem mortalibus adfert,
    crura licet dura compede pulsa sonent.
non tibi sunt tristes curae nec luctus, Osiri,
    sed chorus et cantus et levis aptus amor,
sed varii flores et frons redimita corymbis,
    fusa sed ad teneros lutea palla pedes
et Tyriae vestes et dulcis tibia cantu
    et levis occultis conscia cista sacris.
huc ades et centum ludis Geniumque choreis
    concelebra et multo tempora funde mero:
illius et nitido stillent unguenta capillo,
    et capite et collo mollia serta gerat.
sic venias hodierne: tibi dem turis honores,
    liba et Mopsopio dulcia melle feram.

at tibi succrescat proles quae facta parentis
    augeat et circa stet veneranda senem.
nec taceat monumenta viae quem Tuscula tellus
    candidaque antiquo detinet Alba lare.
namque opibus congesta tuis hic glarea dura
    sternitur, hic apta iungitur arte silex.
te canit agricola, magna cum venerit urbe
    serus inoffensum rettuleritque pedem.

at tu, Natalis multos celebrande per annos,
    candidior semper candidiorque veni.

For him the ripe grape-bunches first gave up their
  delightful juice,
      Pressed out by uncouth treading feet.
Their liquor taught voices to rise and fall in song,
Stirred ignorant limbs into true rhythm.
As Bacchus, he bestows upon the farmer's breast,
Spent from heavy work, release from sorrows;
And as Bacchus, brings a respite to despondent mortals,
Though hard shackles clank when a leg is moved.
For you, Osiris, bitter cares and grief aren't suitable,
But dancing, singing, light-hearted love, rainbows of flowers,
Foreheads crowned with clusters of ivy berries,
Saffron robes trailing at youthful feet,
Tyrian clothes, the bone-flute sweet with song,
And the light wicker box, privy to secret holy things.
Come to us here, in a hundred games and dances honor
The Guardian Spirit and lave his brow with copious wine.
Let unguents trickle down his glistening hair
And graceful garlands hang round his head and neck.
May you come thus today, that I may offer
Incense to you and give holy cakes, sweet with Attic honey.

For you, Messalla, may sons grow up to augment their
  father's deeds
And, worthy of great honor, companion your old age.
And let him who is detained by Tusculan fields and the
  ancient hearth
In gleaming Alba not be silent as to your memorial road.
For here, built by your wealth, lime-hardened gravel is laid,
And paving stones with expert art conjoined.
The farmer will praise you, when he comes from the great city
By night and gets home without a stumbled foot.

So come, Birth Spirit, join your festival year after year,
Ever more shining, always more joyous and bright!

I, 8

Non ego celari possum quid nutus amantis
  quidve ferant miti lenia verba sono.
nec mihi sunt sortes nec conscia fibra deorum,
  praecinit eventus nec mihi cantus avis:
ipsa Venus magico religatum bracchia nodo
  perdocuit multis non sine verberibus.

desine dissimulare: deus crudelius urit
  quos videt invitos succubuisse sibi.

quid tibi nunc molles prodest coluisse capillos
  saepeque mutatas disposuisse comas,
quid fuco splendente genas ornare, quid ungues
  artificis docta subsecuisse manu?
frustra iam vestes, frustra mutantur amictus
  ansaque compressos colligat arta pedes.
illa placet, quamvis inculto venerit ore
  nec nitidum tarda compserit arte caput.

num te carminibus, num te pallentibus herbis
  devovit tacito tempore noctis anus?
cantus vicinis fruges traducit ab agris,
  cantus et iratae detinet anguis iter,
cantus et e curru Lunam deducere temptat,
  et faceret, si non aera repulsa sonent.
quid queror heu misero carmen nocuisse, quid herbas?
  forma nihil magicis utitur auxiliis:

I, 8

I cannot keep from seeing what a lover's nods
Or gentle words, softly whispered, reveal.
And yet no fortune-telling do I use,
Nor entrails privy to the gods' intent,
And no bird songs herald to me what's about to happen:
Venus herself, when she had tied my arms with magic knots,
Taught me well, but not without a lot of whipping.

Stop pretending, Marathus. The Love-god inflames
    more fiercely
Those he sees are reluctant to surrender.

What good is it now to curl your swishing hair,
And often do the tresses in a different style?
What good to primp your cheeks with vivid rouge,
And let your nails be manicured by an expert hand?
No use at all now, changing your robes and mantles,
And your feet are squeezed in shoes with thongs too tight.
You like that girl, though she comes with face untidy
And gives no time or pains to dressing her glossy locks.

Has a witch, by magic charms or herbs that turn you pale,
Enchanted you in the silent hours of night?
Spells transplant the crops from a neighbor's fields,
    Arrest the glide of a furious snake,
And try to drag the Moon down from her chariot, and
    would succeed
        Unless the beaten bronze gongs sounded.
What charms, what herbs, alas, do I complain

sed corpus tetigisse nocet, sed longa dedisse
oscula, sed femori conseruisse femur.

nec tu difficilis puero tamen esse memento;
    persequitur poenis tristia facta Venus.
munera ne poscas: det munera canus amator,
    ut foveat molli frigida membra sinu.
carior est auro iuvenis cui levia fulgent
    ora nec amplexus aspera barba terit.
huic tu candentes umero suppone lacertos,
    et regum magnae despiciantur opes.
at Venus inveniet puero succumbere furtim,
    dum tumet et teneros conserit usque sinus,
et dare anhelanti pugnantibus umida linguis
    oscula et in collo figere dente notas.
non lapis hanc gemmaeque iuvant quae frigore sola
    dormiat et nulli sit cupienda viro.

heu sero revocatur amor seroque iuventas,
    cum vetus infecit cana senecta caput.
tum studium formae est: coma tum mutatur, ut annos
    dissimulet viridi cortice tincta nucis:
tollere tum cura est albos a stirpe capillos
    et faciem dempta pelle referre novam.
at tu dum primi floret tibi temporis aetas
    utere: non tardo labitur illa pede.

neu Marathus torque: puero quae gloria victo est?
    in veteres esto dura, puella, senes.
parce precor tenero: non illi sontica causa est,
    sed nimius luto corpora tingit amor.
vel miser absenti maestas quam saepe querellas
    conicit et lacrimis omnia plena madent!

Have hurt poor me? Beauty needs no help from sorcery.
What hurts is your touching the body, giving the
    lingering kiss,
        And twining together thigh to thigh.

Yet remember, my girl, don't be hard-hearted to this boy.
Venus prosecutes callous deeds with penalties.
Don't ask for presents. Let your hoary lover give the gifts
For snuggling cold bony limbs against your soft embrace.
Dearer than gold the boy whose face glows smooth
With no rough whiskers scratching when you hug.
        Under his shoulders slip your white arms
And gaze down on a king's most precious treasure.
Venus will concoct ways to couple secretly with the boy
While he, upsurging, keeps plowing and sowing your
    soft furrow,
And panting, gives wet kisses with your fighting tongues
        And bites teeth-prints upon your neck.
Jewels and pearls won't ravish her who lies in bed,
Cold and lonely, and stirs desire in no man.

Too late, alas, too late, to call back love and youth
When ashen age has spread your head with white.
Then we study the tricks of beauty—the hair is dyed
With stain from green nut-hulls to hide the years;
Then it's our concern to pluck out white hairs by the roots,
And show a brand-new face with wrinkled hide all gone.
But now while youth unfolds its first spring flowers,
Enjoy it: not on lingering feet does it slip away.

Don't torture Marathus. What glory in crushing a boy?
        Be ruthless with tough old rakes, my girl.
Spare this tender lad, I beg; he's not a medical case,
But too much loving tinges his skin with yellow.
How often the poor boy hurls mournful complaints at the
    truant,
And soaks the whole place with a flood of tears!

"quid me spernis?" ait. "poterat custodia vinci:
    ipse dedit cupidis fallere posse deus.
nota Venus furtiva mihi est, ut lenis agatur
    spiritus, ut nec dent oscula rapta sonum:
et possum media quamvis obrepere nocte
    et strepitu nullo clam reserare fores.
quid prosunt artes, miserum si spernit amantem
    et fugit ex ipso saeva puella toro?
vel cum promittit, subito sed perfida fallit,
    est mihi nox multis evigilanda malis.
dum mihi venturam fingo, quodcumque movetur,
    illius credo tunc sonuisse pedes."

desistas lacrimare, puer: non frangitur illa,
    et tua iam fletu lumina fessa tument.

oderunt, Pholoë, moneo, fastidia divi,
    nec prodest sanctis tura dedisse focis.
hic Marathus quondam miseros ludebat amantes.
    nescius ultorem post caput esse deum:
saepe etiam lacrimas fertur risisse dolentis
    et cupidum ficta detinuisse mora:
nunc omnes odit fastus, nunc displicet illi
    quaecumque opposita est ianua dura sera.

at te poena manet, ni desinis esse superba.
    quam cupies votis hunc revocare diem!

"Why do you spurn me?" he wails. "You could have foiled
   your guards.
The Love-god himself gives lovers power to dodge them.
I know the tricks of secret sex-play, the ways of breathing soft
      And stealing kisses without a sound.
And even in the midnight hours I can creep up
And, known to none, unlock a door with not one rattle.
What good this science, if the stricken lover is spurned
And the cruel girl bolts out of the very bed?
Or when she makes a date but, two-faced, suddenly cheats me,
And my night is a sleepless waiting, charged with anguish?
      When I'm expecting her to come,
The tiniest rustle seems to me the sound of her feet."

Leave off your weeping, my boy; it will not soften her.
And your weary eyes already are swollen from tears.

Pholoë, I warn you, the gods detest disdain,
And offering incense at their holy altars is no help.
This very Marathus used to jeer at wretched lovers,
Not knowing the god of vengeance was breathing down
   his neck.
They say he also often laughed at anguished tears
And balked a lover's urge with sham delay.
      Now he hates all arrogance, now
He fumes at every door shut fast to him at night.

So punishment waits for you, wench, unless you leave off pride.
Then how you'll wish by prayers to call this day back again!

85496

I,9

Quid mihi, si fueras miseros laesurus amores,
    foedera per divos, clam violanda, dabas?
a miser, et si quis primo periuria celat,
    sera tamen tacitis poena venit pedibus.
parcite, caelestes: aequum est impune licere
    numina formosis laedere vestra semel.

lucra petens habili tauros adiungit aratro
    et durum terrae rusticus urget opus,
lucra petituras freta per parentia ventis
    ducunt instabiles sidera certa rates:
muneribus meus est captus puer. at deus illa
    in cinerem et liquidas munera vertat aquas.
iam mihi persolvet poenas, pulvisque decorem
    detrahet et ventis horrida facta coma,
uretur facies, urentur sole capilli,
    deteret invalidos et via longa pedes.

admonui quotiens "auro ne pollue formam:
    saepe solent auro multa subesse mala.
divitiis captus si quis violavit amorem,
    asperaque est illi difficilisque Venus.
ure meum potius flamma caput et pete ferro
    corpus et intorto verbere terga seca.
nec tibi celandi spes sit peccare paranti:
    est deus occultos qui vetat esse dolos.
ipse deus tacito permisit saepe ministro
    ederet ut multo libera verba mero:

I,9

Why, if you were resolved to blight my joyless love,
Did you give me your pledge of faithfulness on the gods,
    Yet break it behind my back?
Poor boy, though your perjury be hidden a while,
Nonetheless in time Vengeance comes on silent feet.
Spare him, heavenly powers! It's only fair that beauty may sin,
Just once, against your will and go unpunished.

Pursuit of wealth! For this the farmer yokes to a handy plow
His oxen and sticks to hard work in the fields.
In quest of wealth, across wind-governed seas
The pitching vessels steer a course by the fixed stars.
    By money my boy has been captured.
Oh gods, turn all his gain to ashes and streams of water!
Soon he'll pay in full for the hurt to me: dirty work
Will sap his beauty, the wind turn shaggy his curls,
The sun will blister his face, scorch his hair,
    Long marches will cripple his delicate feet.

How many times I've warned: "Don't soil your beauty
    with gold.
Under gold it's usual often to find many evils.
If anyone, enslaved to wealth, breaks faith with love,
Venus will use him fiercely, without mercy.
But burn my head, instead of his, with flames,
Pierce my breast with a sword, cut my back with plaited whips.
But nurse no hope, my boy, to hide your plots for sinning.
The god who lets no guilt remain concealed knows all.
That god himself set bottles before the mum accomplice

ipse deus somno domitos emittere vocem
  iussit et invitos facta tegenda loqui."

haec ego dicebam: nunc me flevisse loquentem,
  nunc pudet ad teneros procubuisse pedes.
tunc mihi iurabas nullo te divitis auri
  pondere, non gemmis, vendere velle fidem,
non tibi si pretium Campania terra daretur,
  non tibi si Bacchi cura Falernus ager.
illis eriperes verbis mihi sidera caeli
  lucere et puras fulminis esse vias.
quin etiam flebas: at non ego fallere doctus
  tergebam umentes credulus usque genas.

quid faciam, nisi et ipse fores in amore puellae?
  sed precor exemplo sit levis illa tuo.
o quotiens, verbis ne quisquam conscius esset,
  ipse comes multa lumina nocte tuli!
saepe insperanti venit tibi munere nostro
  et latuit clausas post adoperta fores.
tum miser interii, stulte confisus amari:
  nam poteram ad laqueos cautior esse tuos.
quin etiam attonita laudes tibi mente canebam,
  et me nunc nostri Pieridumque pudet.
illa velim rapida Vulcanus carmina flamma
  torreat et liquida deleat amnis aqua.
tu procul hinc absis cui formam vendere cura est
  et pretium plena grande referre manu.

To make him babble a full confession in his cups;
The same god bids the sleep-sealed voice to speak
    and unwillingly
        Tell of the deeds it would like to keep dark."

All this I used to say. Now I'm ashamed that I sobbed
    my words
And flung myself down at your boyish feet.
Each time you'd swear you never would sell your constancy
For any amount of precious gold or pearls,
Not you, though Campania's fields be given as payment,
Or Falernian vineyards where Bacchus is overseer.
With such words you could have stripped me of belief
    that stars
Shine in the sky and lightning makes a dazzling streak.
And oh, you'd even weep: but I, untutored in deceit
And credulous, would always dry your streaming cheeks.

What wouldn't I do, if you yourself were not in love—
    with a girl!
I pray she'll be fickle, with you as model, be fickle.
Oh how often, so none should know of your courtship,
I myself have gone with you as lantern-boy
In far-spent night; how often, when you'd lost hope,
I contrived that she come and wait hidden behind the
    bolted door.
Then, wretched me, was I lost, stupidly sure I was loved;
For I might have been more cautious about your snares.
Instead, with reason stunned, I even wrote poems to
    praise you,
        But now I'm ashamed of myself and the Muses.
May Vulcan burn those songs with savage flames
        And rivers dissolve them in currents of water.
Go, get away from me, boy, whose concern is selling
    your beauty
And coming home with your hands full of fat wages.

at te qui puerum donis corrumpere es ausus
   rideat adsiduis uxor inulta dolis,
et cum furtivo iuvenem lassaverit usu,
   tecum interposita languida veste cubet.
semper sint externa tuo vestigia lecto,
   et pateat cupidis semper aperta domus:
nec lasciva soror dicatur plura bibisse
   pocula vel plures emeruisse viros.
illam saepe ferunt convivia ducere Baccho
   dum rota Luciferi provocet orta diem:
illa nulla queat melius consumere noctem
   aut operum varias disposuisse vices.
at tua perdidicit: nec tu, stultissime, sentis,
   cum tibi non solita corpus ab arte movet.
tune putas illam pro te disponere crines
   aut tenues denso pectere dente comas?
ista haec persuadet facies, auroque lacertos
   vinciat et Tyrio prodeat apta sinu?
non tibi, sed iuveni cuidam vult bella videri,
   devoveat pro quo remque domumque tuam.
nec facit hoc vitio, sed corpora foeda podagra
   et senis amplexus culta puella fugit.

huic tamen accubuit noster puer: hunc ego credam
   cum trucibus Venerem iungere posse feris.
blanditiasne meas aliis tu vendere es ausus,
   tune aliis demens oscula ferre mea?
tum flebis, cum me vinctum puer alter habebit
   et geret in regno regna superba tuo.
at tua tum me poena iuvet, Venerique merenti
   fixa notet casus aurea palma meos:

HANC TIBI FALLACI RESOLVTVS AMORE TIBVLLVS
DEDICAT ET GRATA SIS, DEA, MENTE ROGAT.

But as for you, old man who dares corrupt my boy with gifts,
May your wife without punishment ridicule you with
    endless intrigues,
And after she's drained her lover with secret bawdry,
Stretch, fagged out, beside you with sheets tucked in between.
May the stains of outsiders be always wet on your bed,
And your house always open, free and easy, to lechers.
Nor let it be said that your lascivious sister outguzzles her
In goblets of wine, or wilts more virile mates.
She, they say, often keeps her drunken orgies going
Till Lucifer's chariot wheels call forth the dawn.
No one could squander the nighttime better than she
Or better arrange the diverse positions of love's performance.
And your wife also has thoroughly learned; yet you, utter fool,
Never see her body squirming in tricks untried on you.
Do you imagine she's dressing her coiffure
And combing her hair with a fine-toothed comb for you?
Does such beauty as *yours* move her to band her arms with gold
And parade the streets decked out in Tyrian robes?
She wants to look lovely, but not to you—to a youth
For whom she'd damn your fortune and family too.
She would not do so out of vice; but this elegant girl
Recoils from filthy, gouty limbs and an old man's hugging.

    And yet my boy has done it with him.
I believe he could even roll and rut with a savage beast.
Crazy boy, do you dare sell others the fondling I should have,
    Give others the kisses that are mine?
You'll weep when another lad holds me in bonds
And wields the proud scepter in your former realm.
And then I'll enjoy your punishment and write on a
    golden palm-leaf,
Raised to Venus for her services, my story:

THIS, O GODDESS, TIBULLUS, FREED FROM DECEITFUL LOVE,
DEDICATES TO THEE AND PRAYS THOU BE GRATEFULLY
    DISPOSED.

I, 10

Quis fuit horrendos primus qui protulit enses?
  quam ferus et vere ferreus ille fuit!
tum caedes hominum generi, tum proelia nata,
  tum brevior dirae mortis aperta via est.
an nihil ille miser meruit, nos ad mala nostra
  vertimus in saevas quod dedit ille fesra?
divitis hoc vitium est auri, nec bella fuerunt,
  faginus astabat cum scyphus ante dapes.
non arces, non vallus erat, somnumque petebat
  securus varias dux gregis inter oves.
tunc mihi vita foret, vulgi nec tristia nossem
  arma nec audissem corde micante tubam.
nunc ad bella trahor, et iam quis forsitan hostis
  haesura in nostro tela gerit latere.

sed patrii servate Lares: aluistis et idem,
  cursarem vestros cum tener ante pedes.
neu pudeat prisco vos esse e stipite factos:
  sic veteris sedes incoluistis avi.
tunc melius tenuere fidem, cum paupere cultu
  stabat in exigua ligneus aede deus.
hic placatus erat, seu quis libaverat uvam,
  seu dederat sanctae spicea serta comae:
atque aliquis voti compos liba ipse ferebat
  postque comes purum filia parva favum.
at nobis aerata, Lares, depellite tela,

*　　*　　*　　*　　*　　*

I, 10

Who was the man that invented the terrible sword?
How fierce he was, as if truly forged of iron himself!
Then slaughter and strife were born for the race of men,
And then a quicker road to grisly death was cut.
     But the wretch may not deserve our blame;
Don't we pervert to our woe what he gave us for
    savage beasts?
This is the curse of golden greed; for long ago
When beechwood cups stood by our food, there were no wars.
There were no forts or ramparts, and the carefree herdsman
    sought sleep
Among his variegated sheep. I wish I'd lived in those days,
    Never known grim war and rabble troops,
Never heard, with heart aquiver, the bugle call.
Now I'm dragged off to war and perhaps some foe
Already bears the spear that is to stick in my side.

Hearth-gods of my fathers, save me. You also fostered me
When I in childhood scampered about your feet.
And don't be ashamed that you're carved from an
    old tree-trunk:
As such you dwelt in my ancestors' home in years gone by.
Then faith was better kept, when the wooden god,
Poorly arrayed, was standing in his little fane.
He was pleased if someone had offered him first grapes
    Or bestowed a corn wreath on his sacred head.
And any whose prayer was fulfilled would himself bring
    holy cakes,
With his little daughter behind, bearing pure honeycombs.

hostiaque e plena rustica porcus hara.
hanc pura cum veste sequar myrtoque canistra
vincta geram, myrto vinctus et ipse caput.

sic placeam vobis: alius sit fortis in armis,
    sternat et adversos Marte favente duces,
ut mihi potanti possit sua dicere facta
    miles et in mensa pingere castra mero.
quis furor est atram bellis arcessere Mortem?
    imminet et tacito clam venit illa pede.
non seges est infra, non vinea culta, sed audax
    Cerberus et Stygiae navita turpis aquae:
illic perscissisque genis ustoque capillo
    errat ad obscuros pallida turba lacus.
quam potius laudandus hic est quem prole parata
    occupat in parva pigra senecta casa!
ipse suas sectatur oves, at filius agnos,
    et calidam fesso comparat uxor aquam.
sic ego sim, liceatque caput candescere canis,
    temporis et prisci facta referre senem.

interea Pax arva colat. Pax candida primum
    duxit araturos sub iuga curva boves:
Pax aluit vites et sucos condidit uvae,
    funderet ut nato testa paterna merum:
pace bidens vomerque nitent, at tristia duri
    militis in tenebris occupat arma situs.

     *   *   *   *   *   *

rusticus e lucoque vehit, male sobrius ipse,
    uxorem plaustro progeniemque domum.

Turn aside from me, oh gods, the bronze spears
      And in thanksgiving for my safe return
You'll have a pig, a rustic sacrifice, from the full sty.
Clean-robed, I'll follow it and bear the wicker basket
Bound with myrtle, and have my own head with
      myrtle wreathed.

Let me please you thus: let others be brave in war,
And, helped by Mars, overthrow the enemy leaders,
So that a soldier may tell me, as I drink, his exploits,
And draw on the table the battle-lines in wine.
What madness is this, inviting sable Death by warfare?
It always hovers close and comes unforeseen on silent steps.
There are no grain fields below, no tended vineyards,
But mad-dog Cerberus and the foul boatman of Stygian floods;
There, with sundered jaws and hair singed by pyres,
The bone-white throng roams around the lake of darkness.
Truly, more praiseworthy is he to whom, with
      offspring begotten,
Sluggish old age lays claim in his small farmhouse!
He himself tends the sheep, his son the lambs,
And his wife brings in hot water for their aching joints.
Thus let me live, let my head at length with gray hair shine,
Let an old man tell over his tale of bygone times.

Meanwhile let Peace till my fields. White-robed Peace
First put steers beneath the curving yoke to plow;
Peace made the vines to grow and put up grape juice
So wine for his son might pour from the father's jugs.
In peacetime the hoe and plowshare gleam; while the
      grim armor
Of rough soldiers is ravaged by rust in the dark.
When Peace rules, festivals honor the harvest gods,
And peasants leap the bonfires, sing and pass the flagon,
Till the farmer, far from sober himself, drives home
From the sacred wood with wife and children in the cart.

sed Veneris tunc bella calent, scissosque capillos
  femina perfractas conqueriturque fores:
flet teneras subtusa genas: sed victor et ipse
  flet sibi dementes tam valuisse manus.
at lascivus Amor rixae mala verba ministrat,
  inter et iratum lentus utrumque sedet.

a, lapis est ferrumque suam quicumque puellam
  verberat: e caelo deripit ille deos.
sit satis e membris tenuem rescindere vestem,
  sit satis ornatus dissoluisse comae,
sit lacrimas movisse satis: quater ille beatus
  quo tenera irato flere puella potest.
sed manibus qui saevus erit, scutumque sudemque
  is gerat et miti sit procul a Venere.

at nobis, Pax alma, veni spicamque teneto,
  perfluat et pomis candidus ante sinus,

But then the battles of love wax hot.
The woman bewails her snatched-out hair, the shattered doors,
    And, bruised, weeps for her tender cheeks.
Even the victor weeps that his frenzied hands used so
    much force.
And saucy Cupid eggs on the fight with caustic comments,
While he sits indifferent between the furious couple.

The man who'd beat his girl is made of flint and iron;
    He'd drag the gods down from the heavens!
Be satisfied with pulling the thin clothes from her limbs,
    Satisfied with tousling her fine hair-do,
With starting her tears. Blest fourfold is he whose anger
Can make a gentle maiden weep! But he who's fierce with
    his hands
Should bear the shield and pike and shun the ways of
    soft Venus.

Then be with us, nourishing Peace. Lift up the ear of corn
And let the fruits from your white robes flow out before us.

II

MESSALLA
CORNUTUS
NEMESIS
MESSALINUS
MACER
PHRYNE

III

ELEGIES
19 and 20

II, 1

Quisquis adest, faveat: fruges lustramus et agros
　　ritus ut a prisco traditus exstat avo.
Bacche, veni, dulcisque tuis e cornibus uva
　　pendeat, et spicis tempora cinge, Ceres.
luce sacra requiescat humus, requiescat arator,
　　et grave suspenso vomere cesset opus.
solvite vincla iugis: nunc ad praesepia debent
　　plena coronato stare boves capite.
omnia sint operata deo: non audeat ulla
　　lanificam pensis imposuisse manum.
vos quoque abesse procul iubeo, discedat ab aris,
　　cui tulit hesterna gaudia nocte Venus.
casta placent superis: pura cum veste venite
　　et manibus puris sumite fontis aquam.
cernite fulgentes ut eat sacer agnus ad aras
　　vinctaque post olea candida turba comas.

di patrii, purgamus agros, purgamus agrestes:
　　vos mala de nostris pellite limitibus,
neu seges eludat messem fallacibus herbis,
　　neu timeat celeres tardior agna lupos.
tunc nitidus plenis confisus rusticus agris
　　ingeret ardenti grandia ligna foco,
turbaque vernarum, saturi bona signa coloni,
　　ludet et ex virgis exstruet ante casas.

II, 1

Silence, everyone here. We are hallowing our crops and fields
By the rites our ancient sires bequeathed to us.
Bacchus, come, let sweet grapes dangle from your horns;
Come, Ceres, and wreathe your brow with a grain-spike crown.
On this holy day leave earth in peace, let plowhands rest,
And, with the shares hung up, let hard labor stop.
Loosen the ropes from yokes; at the bulging cribs
The oxen now must stand with garlanded heads.
Let everyone serve the god. Let no maiden venture
To set her hand to spinning a stint of wool.
    I command you also to stay far away,
You to whom Venus brought sensual joys last night;
Do not come near the altar. The gods above like purity:
Approach in clean clothing, with clean hands dip
    The water from the spring.
See, how the consecrated lamb moves toward the shining altar,
And the white-clad procession follows with olive twining
    their hair.

"Gods of our fathers, we now atone for farms and
    country folk.
Beyond our boundaries banish all evil powers.
Let planted fields not parry the harvest with cheating blades,
Let our slow lambs not fear the swifter wolves.
In time the well-fed farmer, assured an abundant yield,
    Will heap great logs on the glowing bonfire
And a swarm of house-born slaves, good sign of a
    happy countryman,
Will play games before it and fashion shelters of branches."

eventura precor: viden ut felicibus extis
significet placidos nuntia fibra deos?
nunc mihi fumosos veteris proferte Falernos
consulis et Chio solvite vincla cado.
vina diem celebrent: non festa luce madere
est rubor, errantes et male ferre pedes.
sed "bene Messallam" sua quisque ad pocula dicat,
nomen et absentis singula verba sonent.

gentis Aquitanae celeber Messalla triumphis
et magna intonsis gloria victor avis,
huc ades aspiraque mihi, dum carmine nostro
redditur agricolis gratia caelitibus.

rura cano rurisque deos.   his vita magistris
desuevit querna pellere glande famem:
illi compositis primum docuere tigillis
exiguam viridi fronde operire domum:
illi etiam tauros primi docuisse feruntur
servitium et plaustro supposuisse rotam.
tum victus abiere feri, tum consita pomus,
tum bibit irriguas fertilis hortus aquas,
aurea tum pressos pedibus dedit uva liquores
mixtaque securo est sobria lympha mero.
rura ferunt messes, calidi cum sideris aestu
deponit flavas annua terra comas.
rure levis verno flores apis ingerit alveo,
compleat ut dulci sedula melle favos.
agricola adsiduo primum satiatus aratro
cantavit certo rustica verba pede
et satur arenti primum est modulatus avena
carmen, ut ornatos diceret ante deos,
agricola et minio suffusus, Bacche, rubenti

My prayer's to be answered! Don't you see
How herald filaments in the luck-bringing entrails
Show the gods are pleased? Now bring me the bottle of
    smoky Falernian—
The old vintage—and break the seals from the jars of Chian.
Celebrate this day in wine. It's no disgrace
To get drunk on a holiday and stagger on wobbling feet.
But let everyone shout with each cup: "Health to Messalla!"
And all your speech ring with the name of the absent one.

Messalla, famed for conquest of Aquitanian tribes,
Victorious to the great glory of your uncouth ancestors,
Be with me here and inspire me, while I in my song
Give thanks to the heavenly powers of husbandry.

    I sing of the country and country gods.
On their instruction man quit using acorns to drive out hunger.
They first taught him to roof his lowly house
With bound saplings, thatched with green leaf-fronds.
They're also said to have trained the bull first for servitude
        And set the wheel beneath the cart.
Then savage customs died out, then fruit trees were planted,
And fertile gardens drank from irrigation canals;
Then golden grapes yielded their juices to treading feet,
And sobering water was mixed with cheering wine.
Our fields produce their harvest when in the season's hot glow
Each year the earth is shorn of its yellow mane.
Over meadows in spring the nimble bee brings flower nectar
To the hive and busily fills the combs with sweet honey.
    The farmer, wearied by plowing all day,
First sang rustic songs in proper rhythm,
And after supper played a tune on dried reed pipes
To chant before the gods in their festal dress.
And a farmer, smeared with ruddy cinnabar, O Bacchus,

primus inexperta duxit ab arte choros.
huic datus a pleno, memorabile munus, ovili
    dux pecoris curtas auxerat hircus opes.
rure puer verno primum de flore coronam
    fecit et antiquis imposuit Laribus.
rure etiam teneris curam exhibitura puellis
    molle gerit tergo lucida vellus ovis.
hinc et femineus labor est, hinc pensa colusque,
    fusus et apposito pollice versat opus:
atque aliqua adsiduae textrix operata Minervae
    cantat, et applauso tela sonat latere.

ipse quoque inter agros interque armenta Cupido
    natus et indomitas dicitur inter equas.
illic indocto primum se exercuit arcu:
    ei mihi, quam doctas nunc habet ille manus!
nec pecudes, velut ante, petit: fixisse puellas
    gestit et audaces perdomuisse viros.
hic iuveni detraxit opes, hic dicere iussit
    limen ad iratae verba pudenda senem:
hoc duce custodes furtim transgressa iacentes
    ad iuvenem tenebris sola puella venit
et pedibus praetemptat iter suspensa timore,
    explorat caecas cui manus ante vias.

a miseri, quos hic graviter deus urget! at ille
    felix, cui placidus leniter adflat Amor.
sancte, veni dapibus festis, sed pone sagittas
    et procul ardentes hinc precor abde faces.
vos celebrem cantate deum pecorique vocate

First led the choric dance with unschooled art.
By sacrifice of a notable gift from a full sheepfold—
The billy goat that led the flock—he swelled his
    meager wealth.
A slave boy in the country first wove flower wreaths
In spring and crowned the old domestic gods.
Also in the country the sheep grows downy wool
On its shining back to make more bother for gentle girls.
        And it's the cause of women's labor,
Of masses of wool, of distaff and spindle, with thumb
    in place,
Twirling the work. And some who weave in Minerva's
    constant service
Sing, and the loom rattles with clashings of baked clay weights.

Even Cupid himself, they say, was born among fields and herds,
        Among the unbridled mares.
There he practiced first with his unskilled bow:
Oh my! What skillful hands he has today!
Nor does he aim at cattle as before: he desires
To pierce the girls and tame bold men completely.
        He takes away from youths their wealth,
He makes old men blurt shameful words at an angry
    wench's door.
With him as guide, a girl furtively tiptoes
Over her sleeping guards, creeps alone to a lover at night,
And twitching with fear, feels her way with her feet
And gropes with hand outstretched through the hall she
    cannot see.

Oh wretched those men this god severely besets!
But happy the one whom soft Love sweetly blows upon.
Divine Being, come share our festal banquet.
        But leave your arrows behind, I beg you,
And keep your flaming torch far, far from here.

voce: palam pecori, clam sibi quisque vocet.
aut etiam sibi quisque palam: nam turba iocosa
obstrepit et Phrygio tibia curva sono.

ludite: iam Nox iungit equos, currumque sequuntur
 matris lascivo sidera fulva choro,
postque venit tacitus furvis circumdatus alis
 Somnus et incerto Somnia nigra pede.

II, 2

Dicamus bona verba: venit Natalis ad aras:
 quisquis ades, lingua, vir mulierque, fave.
urantur pia tura focis, urantur odores
 quos tener e terra divite mittit Arabs.
ipse suos Genius adsit visurus honores,
 cui decorent sanctas mollia serta comas.
illius puro destillent tempora nardo,
 atque satur libo sit madeatque mero,
adnuat et, Cornute, tibi quodcumque rogabis.
 en age, quid cessas? adnuit ille: roga.

Sing this renowned god's praise and pray him aloud for
    your herd:
Out loud for the herd, but in a whisper for yourself.
Or even aloud for yourself, for the jocular crowd
And the Phrygian squeal of the curved bone-flute will drown
    it out.

Have fun. Already Night is harnessing her horses, and
    tawny stars
In a frolicking swarm trail after their mother's chariot
And behind them, silent, encompassed by dusky pinions,
Come Sleep and, on impalpable feet, night-dark Dreams.

II, 2

Let us speak in auspicious words: the Birth Spirit comes to
    the altar.
Whatever men and women are present, please be silent.
        Let holy incense be burnt in its fires,
Let spices be burnt, which the languid Arab sends from his
    opulent land.
Let the Genius himself come forth to see the offerings to him
Whose sacred hair our graceful garlands adorn.
        Let his temples drip with pure spikenard;
Let him be stuffed with holy cakes, besotted with neat wine.
Then must he agree, Cornutus, to what you ask.
Quick, do it—why dillydally? He nods assent—ask him!

auguror, uxoris fidos optabis amores:
   iam reor hoc ipsos edidicisse deos.
nec tibi malueris totum quaecumque per orbem
   fortis arat valido rusticus arva bove,
nec tibi, gemmarum quidquid felicibus Indis
   nascitur, Eoi qua maris unda rubet.

vota cadunt: utinam strepitantibus advolet alis
   flavaque coniugio vincula portet Amor,
vincula quae maneant semper dum tarda senectus
   inducat rugas inficiatque comas.

hic veniat Natalis avis prolemque ministret,
   ludat et ante tuos turba novella pedes.

II, 3

Rura meam, Cornute, tenent villaeque puellam:
   ferreus est, heu heu, quisquis in urbe manet.
ipsa Venus latos iam nunc migravit in agros,
   verbaque aratoris rustica discit Amor.
o ego, cum aspicerem dominam, quam fortiter illic
   versarem valido pingue bidente solum
agricolaeque modo curvum sectarer aratrum,
   dum subigunt steriles arva serenda boves!
nec quererer quod sol graciles exureret artus,
   laederet et teneras pussula rupta manus.

My prediction is, you'll wish your wife's love ever true.
By now I'd think the gods would know that prayer by heart.
You'd never choose for yourself all the world-wide fields
Which robust farmers plow with stalwart oxen,
Not for yourself all the pearls produced in favored India
  Where tides of the Eastern Sea run red.

Your prayer is granted. May Love on murmuring wings
Fly to you and wrap your marriage in golden cords,
  Bonds that will endure forever,
Though creeping old age spread wrinkles on your cheeks
  And whiten your hair.

Thus let it befall, Birth Spirit, give them long life, children,
And a brood of the children's toddlers to play at your feet.

II, 3

Fields and country villas, Cornutus, restrain my sweetheart.
Whoever stays in town, alas, is made of iron.
Venus herself has now moved to the broad plantations,
And Cupid's learning the rustic speech of yokels.
  Even I, while I might gaze on my mistress,
Would gamely till the rich soil there with a stout hoe
  And follow the curve-handled plow like a farmer
As barren oxen harrowed the land for sowing.
I'd not complain when the sun burned my slender limbs
And broken blisters hurt my tender hands.

pavit et Admeti tauros formosus Apollo,
   nec cithara intonsae profueruntve comae,
nec potuit curas sanare salubribus herbis:
   quidquid erat medicae vicerat artis amor.
ipse deus solitus stabulis expellere vaccas

     *   *   *   *   *   *

et miscere novo docuisse coagula lacte,
   lacteus et mixtu subriguisse liquor.
tunc fiscella levi detexta est vimine iunci,
   raraque per nexus est via facta sero.
o quotiens illo vitulum gestante per agros
   dicitur occurrens erubuisse soror!
o quotiens ausae, caneret dum valle sub alta,
   rumpere mugitu carmina docta boves!
saepe duces trepidis petiere oracula rebus,
   venit et a templis irrita turba domum:
saepe horrere sacros doluit Latona capillos,
   quos admirata est ipsa noverca prius.
quisquis inornatumque caput crinesque solutos
   aspiceret, Phoebi quaereret ille comam.
Delos ubi nunc, Phoebe, tua est, ubi Delphica Pytho?
   nempe Amor in parva te iubet esse casa.

felices olim, Veneri cum fertur aperte
   servire aeternos non puduisse deos,
fabula nunc ille est: sed cui sua cura puella est
   fabula sit mavult quam sine amore deus.

at tu, quisquis is es cui tristi fronte Cupido
   imperat, ut nostra sint tua castra domo

     *   *   *   *   *   *

In pastures handsome Apollo herded the bulls of Admetus;
Neither his lyre nor uncut hair helped win his desire.
Even he couldn't heal his pangs by salubrious herbs.
Love had conquered all his powers of medical arts.
This god used to drive the cows out from the stables,
The story goes, and milk them in the farmyard,
    And explained how to mix curds in fresh milk
So that the milky fluid coagulated in the process.
Then little baskets were woven from soft stems of rushes
With spaces left in the plaits for whey to drip.
Oh how often, as he carried a calf across the fields,
His sister, they say, blushed with shame at meeting him!
Oh how often, while he crooned in crag-shadowed vales,
Cows had the nerve to puncture his gifted songs with mooing!
Commanders often sought his oracle in critical matters
    And the group went home from his temple unanswered.
Often Latona grieved that his sacred hair was shaggy,
    Which even his stepmother had admired before.
Whoever beheld that uncombed head of bristling tufts
Surely wondered what had happened to Phoebus's curls.
Where now, Apollo, is your shrine of Delos,
    Where that one of Delphic Pytho?
Indeed Love makes you live in a humble hut.

Happy was man long ago when they say the eternal gods
Were not ashamed to be slaves to Venus in sight of all.
Today he's a scandal: but he who's in love with his girl
Would rather be a scandal than a god without a love.

As for you, whoever you are, whom headstrong Cupid
Orders to pitch your camp in my domain,
[Though helpless before that god and victor in my stead,
Beware a future rival to rout you with greater riches.]*

  * Conjectural lines for hiatus in Latin text.

ferrea non Venerem sed praedam saecula laudant:
  praeda tamen multis est operata malis.
praeda feras acies cinxit discordibus armis:
  hinc cruor, hinc caedes mors propiorque venit.
praeda vago iussit geminare pericula ponto,
  bellica cum dubiis rostra dedit ratibus.
praedator cupit immensos obsidere campos,
  ut multa innumera iugera pascat ove:
cui lapis externus curae est, urbisque tumultu
  portatur validis mille columna iugis,
claudit et indomitum moles mare, lentus ut intra
  neglegat hibernas piscis adesse minas.
at tibi laeta trahant Samiae convivia testae
  fictaque Cumana lubrica terra rota.

heu heu divitibus video gaudere puellas:
  iam veniant praedae, si Venus optat opes,
ut mea luxuria Nemesis fluat utque per urbem
  incedat donis conspicienda meis.
illa gerat vestes tenues quas femina Coa
  texuit, auratas disposuitque vias:
illi sint comites fusci quos India torret,
  solis et admotis inficit ignis equis:
illi selectos certent praebere colores
  Africa puniceum purpureumque Tyros.

  *   *   *   *   *   *

nota loquor: regnum ipse tenet quem saepe coegit
  barbara gypsatos ferre catasta pedes.
at tibi dura seges, Nemesim qui abducis ab urbe,
  persolvat nulla semina certa fide.
et tu, Bacche tener, iucundae consitor uvae,
  tu quoque devotos, Bacche, relinque lacus.

This Age of Iron gives honor not to love but to plunder.
    Yet plunder is snarled with many evils.
Plunder buckles the weapons of war on savage armies;
From this do carnage, gore and death more closely touch us.
It made man double the dangers of the tossing seas
By fixing battle-rams on the shaky galleys.
The plunderer yearns to possess unbounded plains
That he may graze great herds of sheep on countless acres.
Imported marble is his craze, and through the uproar of the city
His column is hauled by a thousand yokes of stout oxen;
And he cages the untameable sea within a mole,
So that the phlegmatic fish inside may disdain
    The threat of coming storms.
But for me, let my pleasant meals come ever on Samian ware
Or clay once slick and molded on Cumaean potters' wheels.

Alas, ah me! I see too well that girls love riches.
Then let me plunder, if Love insists on wealth.
Thus may my Nemesis stream with gaudy frills and through
    the city
Parade and preen, stared at by all because of my gifts.
Let her drip with the filmy robes some woman in Cos
Has woven and spangled with golden stripes.
Let her have the swarthy lackeys, scorched in India,
Burnt by the Sun's fire when its horses galloped near.
To furnish her choicest dyes, let Africa's scarlet
    Contend with the purple of Tyre.

What I say is no secret. That very man rules love's kingdom
Who time and again has been forced to move
His gypsum-coated feet across barbarian slave-blocks.
To you, who steal my Nemesis from town, may Earth
Deny returns on the seed invested in your stony fields.
And you, boyish Bacchus, planter of the delightful grapevines,

haud impune licet formosas tristibus agris
abdere: non tanti sunt tua musta, pater.

o valeant fruges, ne sint modo rure puellae:
glans alat, et prisco more bibantur aquae.
glans aluit veteres, et passim semper amarunt:
quid nocuit sulcos non habuisse satos?
tunc quibus aspirabat Amor praebebat aperte
mitis in umbrosa gaudia valle Venus.
nullus erat custos, nulla exclusura dolentes
ianua: si fas est, mos precor ille redi.

*   *   *   *   *   *

horrida villosa corpora veste tegant.
nunc si clausa mea est, si copia rara videndi,
heu miserum, laxam quid iuvat esse togam?

ducite: ad imperium dominae sulcabimus agros:
non ego me vinclis verberibusque nego.

II,4

Hic mihi servitium video dominamque paratam:
iam mihi, libertas illa paterna, vale.
servitium sed triste datur, teneorque catenis,

You too, Bacchus, neglect his accursed vats.
No man may carry off fair girls to dismal farms
And go unpunished. Your new wine, lord, isn't worth
    that much.

Let the crops go hang, unless girls keep away from the farms!
We'll feed on acorns and drink water in primitive style.
Acorns fed the ancients and they always
      Made love all over the place;
How were they hurt by having no planted furrows?
In that age gracious Venus granted those whom Cupid inspired
      Unhidden delights in shady valleys.
No watchmen existed, no doors to be shut on aching lovers.
Gods willing, I pray this custom return.
[Let the power of Love dissolve all bolts and keys,]*
And rugged bodies be covered with shaggy pelts.
For now, if my love's locked in, if my chance of seeing
    her is rare,
What pleasure to me, poor wretch, is a billowing toga?

Lead me away. I'll plow the fields at my mistress's commands
And never shall I shrink from her chains and lashes.

   * Conjectural line for hiatus in Latin text.

II,4

I see enslavement and a mistress closing upon me here.
Goodbye for me now, that former freedom of my fathers!
My fate is bondage—dismal, too. I'm kept in chains,

et numquam misero vincla remittit Amor,
et seu quid merui seu quid peccavimus, urit.
uror, io, remove, saeva puella, faces.

o ego ne possim tales sentire dolores,
    quam mallem in gelidis montibus esse lapis,
stare vel insanis cautes obnoxia ventis,
    naufraga quam vasti tunderet unda maris!
nunc et amara dies et noctis amarior umbra est:
    omnia nunc tristi tempora felle madent.
nec prosunt elegi nec carminis auctor Apollo:
    illa cava pretium flagitat usque manu.

ite procul, Musae, si non prodestis amanti:
    non ego vos, ut sint bella canenda, colo,
nec refero solisque vias et qualis, ubi orbem
    complevit, versis Luna recurrit equis.
ad dominam faciles aditus per carmina quaero:
    ite procul, Musae, si nihil ista valent.

at mihi per caedem et facinus sunt dona paranda,
    ne iaceam clausam flebilis ante domum:
aut rapiam suspensa sacris insignia fanis:
    sed Venus ante alios est violanda mihi.
illa malum facinus suadet dominamque rapacem
    dat mihi: sacrilegas sentiat illa manus.
o pereat quicumque legit viridesque smaragdos
    et niveam Tyrio murice tingit ovem.
hic dat avaritiae causas et Coa puellis
    vestis et e rubro lucida concha mari.
haec fecere malas: hinc clavim ianua sensit
    et coepit custos liminis esse canis.
sed pretium si grande feras, custodia victa est
    nec prohibent claves et canis ipse tacet.

And Cupid never loosens the fetters on his victim,
And whether I deserve it or have done no wrong,
    He burns me. Help! I'm burning up!
    Cruel girl, take his torch away.

Oh, if I might just not feel such deep anguish;
How much I'd rather be a stone on frosty peaks,
Or be a crag exposed to violent winds,
Pounded by shipwrecking waves of abysmal seas!
Now day is bitter and shades of night more bitter still,
    For each moment brims with tearful gall.
There's no help in elegies, nor in Apollo, father of song.
    Her cupped hand is always demanding cash.

Leave me, Muses, if you can't help a lover.
I give you worship not so I may write an epic,
    And picture the path of the Sun
And how the Moon when her orbit is run, with horses turned,
Drives back. Through poems I seek a ready sweet access to
    my mistress.
Go from me, Muses, if poems have no such power.

Yet I, by crime, by murder, must get my hands on some money,
Lest I lie in tears before a locked-up house.
Or I must steal the hallowed emblems from holy temples.
But that of Venus before all others must I profane:
She provokes my wicked deed, for she gives me a
    greedy mistress;
    Let her suffer my sacrilegious hands.
A plague on anyone who collects green emeralds
    And dyes white fleece with Tyrian purple.
This breeds up spurs to greed in girls, and gowns of Cos
    do too,
    And lustrous pearls from sun-red seas.
All these have made them evil; for these, the door endures
    a key

heu quicumque dedit formam caelestis avarae,
    quale bonum multis attulit ille malis!
hinc fletus rixaeque sonant, haec denique causa
    fecit ut infamis sic deus esset Amor.

at tibi quae pretio victos excludis amantes
    eripiant partas ventus et ignis opes:
quin tua tunc iuvenes spectent incendia laeti,
    nec quisquam flammae sedulus addat aquam.
seu veniet tibi Mors, nec erit qui lugeat ullus,
    nec qui det maestas munus in exsequias.
at bona quae nec avara fuit, centum licet annos
    vixerit, ardentem flebitur ante rogum:
atque aliquis senior veteres veneratus amores
    annua constructo serta dabit tumulo
et "bene" discedens dicet "placideque quiescas,
    terraque securae sit super ossa levis."

vera quidem moneo, sed prosunt quid mihi vera?
    illius est nobis lege colendus amor.
quin etiam sedes iubeat si vendere avitas,
    ite sub imperium sub titulumque, Lares.
quidquid habet Circe, quidquid Medea veneni,
    quidquid et herbarum Thessala terra gerit,
et quod, ubi indomitis gregibus Venus adflat amores,
    hippomanes cupidae stillat ab inguine equae,
si modo me placido videat Nemesis mea vultu,
    mille alias herbas misceat illa, bibam.

And a dog begins to guard the threshold.
But if you bring a wad of money, the chaperones are won
And locks don't hold and even the dog is silent.
Oh what a prize some god, in giving beauty to a greedy girl,
Bestowed upon a bundle of wickedness!
Because of this sobs and bickerings are heard. In short,
This shows why Cupid now wanders about, ill spoken of.

But you who slam the door on lovers conquered by cash,
May blasts and blazes snatch up the profits you cherish.
      Still worse, may the young men then watch the fire
And not one move a hand to pour water on the flames.
And when Death pounces on you, be there not a soul
To mourn or offer tributes at your gloomy funeral.
But she who was kind and never greedy, though she live
A hundred years, shall have friends to weep at the
      burning pyre.
And some old man, in homage to his love of long ago,
Will place a wreath on her seemly tomb each year
And, as he leaves, will murmur: "Sleep well, sleep in peace.
Let earth lie gently on your bones now free from care."

At least I'm warning of the truth; but how can truth help me?
I must pursue my darling according to her terms.
In fact, if she tells me to sell my ancestral home,
Then go, household gods, at auction and public sale!
Whatever philtres Circe and Medea listed,
      Such herbs as in magic Thessaly grow,
Along with hippomanes that drip from the loins of mares
      in heat
      When Venus piques wild herds to rut,
My Nemesis may brew with countless other simples,
And, if she'll turn on me a gentle gaze, I'll drink them all.

II, 5

Phoebe, fave: novus ingreditur tua templa sacerdos:
  huc age cum cithara carminibusque veni.
nunc te vocales impellere pollice chordas,
  nunc precor ad laudes flectere verba novas.
ipse triumphali devinctus tempora lauro,
  dum cumulant aras, ad tua sacra veni.
sed nitidus pulcherque veni: nunc indue vestem
  sepositam, longas nunc bene pecte comas,
qualem te memorant Saturno rege fugato
  victori laudes concinuisse Iovi.
tu procul eventura vides, tibi deditus augur
  scit bene quid fati provida cantet avis,
tuque regis sortes, per te praesentit aruspex,
  lubrica signavit cum deus exta notis:

te duce Romanos numquam frustrata Sibylla
  abdita quae senis fata canit pedibus.
Phoebe, sacras Messalinum sine tangere chartas
  vatis, et ipse precor quid canat illa doce.

haec dedit Aeneae sortes, postquam ille parentem
  dicitur et raptos sustinuisse Lares:
nec fore credebat Romam, cum maestus ab alto
  Ilion ardentes respiceretque deos.

II, 5

Your favor, Phoebus! A new priest enters into your temple.
I urge you to come here with your lyre and songs.
Now strum your fingers on the sounding strings,
Now tune some verses into loyal praise, I beg.
Come to your rites with forehead encircled by triumphal laurel,
    While they heap your altar with gifts.
But come bright-shining and handsome. Now put on
    the mantle
Expressly reserved, comb well your flowing hair
To look as men remember you when, after King Saturn's rout,
You sang a paean to victorious Jove.
Far in advance you see what's going to happen;
    The augur dedicated to you
Knows well what a bird which foresees the future sings.
And you rule the lots of fate, through you the entrail-reader
Prophesies when a god has printed on slippery innards
    his sign.

With you to guide her, the Sybil who in hexameters sings
Of hidden destiny never tricked the Romans.
Phoebus, let Messalinus touch the holy books
Of the prophetess; and teach him yourself, I beg, her
    song's burden.

She told Aeneas' fortune, after he had borne away
His father, it's said, and the snatched-up household gods.
    But he didn't believe in a Rome to be,
When from the mountain he looked back sorrowfully on Troy
    And its holy shrines in flame.

Romulus aeternae nondum formaverat urbis
   moenia, consorti non habitanda Remo,
sed tunc pascebant herbosa Palatia vaccae
   et stabant humiles in Iovis arce casae.
lacte madens illic suberat Pan ilicis umbrae
   et facta agresti lignea falce Pales,
pendebatque vagi pastoris in arbore votum,
   garrula silvestri fistula sacra deo,
fistula cui semper decrescit arundinis ordo:
   nam calamus cera iungitur usque minor.
at qua Velabri regio patet, ire solebat
   exiguus pulsa per vada linter aqua.
illa saepe gregis diti placitura magistro
   ad iuvenem festa est vecta puella die,
cum qua fecundi redierunt munera ruris,
   caseus et niveae candidus agnus ovis.

"Impiger Aenea, volitantis frater Amoris,
   Troica qui profugis sacra vehis ratibus,
iam tibi Laurentes adsignat Iuppiter agros,
   iam vocat errantes hospita terra Lares.
illic sanctus eris, cum te veneranda Numici
   unda deum caelo miserit indigetem.
ecce super fessas volitat Victoria puppes,
   tandem ad Troianos diva superba venit.
ecce mihi lucent Rutulis incendia castris:
   iam tibi praedico, barbare Turne, necem.
ante oculos Laurens castrum murusque Lavini est
   Albaque ab Ascanio condita Longa duce.
te quoque iam video, Marti placitura sacerdos
   Ilia, Vestales deseruisse focos,
concubitusque tuos furtim vittasque iacentes
   et cupidi ad ripas arma relicta dei.

(Romulus had not yet laid out the eternal city's walls
In which his brother Remus would never live.
But cattle still grazed on the grassy Palatine,
        And mean huts squatted on top of Jove's Hill.
Dripping with milk, Pan stood there in the ilex shade,
And the herd-god Pales too, carved in wood by a rustic blade,
And from the tree ex-votos of roving shepherds hung down—
The warbling pipes, sacred to the sylvan god,
Pipes whose row of reeds ever dwindles, for each cane
        is joined
        By wax to an always shorter one.
And where today the Velabrum quarter lies,
A little dugout used to go paddling across a shallow pond.
Often a girl, alluring to a wealthy cattle king,
Was ferried across on holidays to her lover,
And came back loaded down with the gifts of a
        fruitful farm—
Cheese, and the pure white lamb of a snowy ewe.)

"Energetic Aeneas, far-flying Cupid's brother," (the
        Sybil said)
"To you who bear in your fugitive ships the holy vessels
        of Troy
        Jupiter now awards the Laurentian fields,
Now a hospitable land invites your wandering house-gods.
There you'll become divine when the worshiped waters
        of Numicus
Send you up to heaven, a native-born god.
Look, Victory hovers above the weakened ships;
The haughty goddess comes at last to the Trojans.
Look, before me the fires shine from the red-lit battle camps;
Now, barbarous Turnus, I prophesy death for you.
Before my eyes rise up Laurentum's fort, Lavinium's wall
And Alba Longa, founded by Ascanius, the new chief.
You too, Ilia, priestess marked to take the fancy of Mars,

carpite nunc, tauri, de septem montibus herbas
  dum licet: hic magnae iam locus urbis erit.
Roma, tuum nomen terris fatale regendis,
  qua sua de caelo prospicit arva Ceres,
quaque patent ortus et qua fluitantibus undis
  Solis anhelantes abluit amnis equos.
Troia quidem tunc se mirabitur et sibi dicet
  vos bene tam longa consuluisse via.
vera cano: sic usque sacras innoxia laurus
  vescar, et aeternum sit mihi virginitas."

haec cecinit vates et te sibi, Phoebe, vocavit,
  iactavit fusas et caput ante comas.
quidquid Amalthea, quidquid Marpesia dixit
  Herophile, Phyto Graia quod admonuit,
quasque Aniena sacras Tiburs per flumina sortes
  portarit sicco pertuleritque sinu
(haec fore dixerunt belli mala signa cometen,
  multus ut in terras deplueretque lapis:
atque tubas atque arma ferunt strepitantia caelo
  audita et lucos praecinuisse fugam,
ipsum etiam Solem defectum lumine vidit
  iungere pallentes nubilus annus equos
et simulacra deum lacrimas fudisse tepentes
  fataque vocales praemonuisse boves),
haec fuerant olim: sed tu iam mitis, Apollo,
  prodigia indomitis merge sub aequoribus,
et succensa sacris crepitet bene laurea flammis,
  omine quo felix et sacer annus erit.

I now see leaving your Vestal fires behind;
I see your secret coition, your sacred fillet cast off,
And the armor of the lustful god dropped on the banks.
Now crop the grass on the seven hills, you bulls, while
    you may;
Soon this will be the site of a great city.
Rome, your name is destined to rule the world
As far as Ceres from heaven can look out on her fields,
From the gates that Dawn swings open to where in its
    tossing waves
The Ocean washes the panting horses of the Sun.
        Then shall Troy marvel at its new self,
And confess you showed good counsel in this long journey.
I chant the truth: so may I ever the holy bay-leaf eat
Unharmed, and eternal virginity be mine."

This the seeress sang, and she invoked you, Phoebus,
        And shook her flying hair in her face.
All that the Sybils told—Amalthea, Herophile of Marpessos—
        All that Grecian Pytho warned,
All that the sacred scrolls the Sybil of Tibur
Bore through Anio's flood and kept dry in her bosom foretold
(All said a comet would come, the evil sign of war,
And torrents of stones would rain upon the earth.
Men tell that trumpets and crashing of weapons were heard
    in the skies,
And gods in sacred groves predicted exile.
Even the Sun itself, with failing light, was seen
To harness ghastly horses through the lowering year,
        And statues of gods shed tepid tears,
And cattle forewarned in human speech of doom),
        All this occurred long ago. But Apollo,
Now kind at last, engulf such prodigies in the invincible seas!
Let kindling laurel keenly crackle in holy flames
As the sign of a blest and lucky year to come.

laurus ubi bona signa dedit, gaudete coloni:
    distendet spicis horrea plena Ceres,
oblitus et musto feriet pede rusticus uvas,
    dolia dum magni deficiantque lacus:
ac madidus Baccho sua festa Palilia pastor
    concinet: a stabulis tunc procul este lupi.
ille levis stipulae sollemnis potus acervos
    accendet, flammas transilietque sacras.
et fetus matrona dabit, natusque parenti
    oscula comprensis auribus eripiet,
nec taedebit avum parvo advigilare nepoti
    balbaque cum puero dicere verba senem.
tunc operata deo pubes discumbet in herba,
    arboris antiquae qua levis umbra cadit,
aut e veste sua tendent umbracula sertis
    vincta, coronatus stabit et ante calix.
at sibi quisque dapes et festas exstruet alte
    caespitibus mensas caespitibusque torum.
ingeret hic potus iuvenis maledicta puellae,
    postmodo quae votis irrita facta velit:
nam ferus ille suae plorabit sobrius idem
    et se iurabit mente fuisse mala.

pace tua pereant arcus pereantque sagittae,
    Phoebe, modo in terris erret inermis Amor.
ars bona: sed postquam sumpsit sibi tela Cupido,
    heu heu quam multis ars dedit illa malum!
et mihi praecipue. iaceo cum saucius annum
    et faveo morbo, cum iuvat ipse dolor,
usque cano Nemesim, sine qua versus mihi nullus
    verba potest iustos aut reperire pedes.

When the laurel has shown good omens, rejoice, all farmers!
Ceres will swell your loaded barns with grain,
And peasants, smeared with must, will tread the grapes
    Till the huge vats and casks are swamped.
And the wine-soaked shepherd will honor in song his own
    feast-day for Pales.
Then, you wolves, keep away from the stables.
Drunk, he'll set the light straw piles on fire, as customary,
    And leap across the sacred flames.
Then his wife will give birth, and the boy, playing jug,
Will grab his father's ears and sip a stolen kiss.
And grandfather won't be bored to nurse his small grandson
And, old as he is, make babytalk with the child.
Then, in the god's homage, people will lie on the grass
Where the dappling shade of an ancient tree falls around,
    Or raise up bowers of their garments,
Bound with garlands, and even the wine cups will be
    crowned with flowers.
And each will heap high for himself the feast of the picnic
On tables of turf with couches of grassy greensward.
Here the drunken youth will pour curses on his sweetheart,
Actions which later on he'll want wiped out by prayers;
    For the man who's brutal to his girl
Will weep when sober and swear he was out of his mind.

A special favor, Phoebus! Let bows come unstrung and
    arrows splinter
So Cupid may rove the earth without a weapon.
It's an honest sport; but since he took up shooting darts,
Alas, how much hurt that same sport has brought to
    many men!
    And particularly me. Wounded
I've lain lovesick for a year, and still (I cherish my ailment,
Since even its pain is joy) I always sing of Nemesis,
Without whom not a poem of mine can find the words or
    proper meter.

at tu (nam divum servat tutela poetas)
    praemoneo, vati parce, puella, sacro,
ut Messalinum celebrem, cum praemia belli
    ante suos currus oppida victa feret,
ipse gerens lauros, lauro devinctus agresti
    miles "io" magna voce "triumphe" canet.
tunc Messalla meus pia det spectacula turbae
    et plaudat curru praetereunte pater.

adnue: sic tibi sint intonsi, Phoebe, capilli,
    sic tua perpetuo sit tibi casta soror.

II, 6

Castra Macer sequitur: tenero quid fiet Amori?
    sit comes et collo fortiter arma gerat?
et seu longa virum terrae via seu vaga ducent
    aequora, cum telis ad latus ire volet?
ure, puer, quaeso, tua qui ferus otia liquit,
    atque iterum erronem sub tua signa voca.
quod si militibus parces, erit hic quoque miles
    ipse levem galea qui sibi portet aquam.
castra peto, valeatque Venus valeantque puellae:
    et mihi sunt vires et mihi facta tuba est.

But you, since a holy providence watches over poets,
I warn you, girl, don't injure this hallowed singer,
          That I may praise Messalinus some day
When he drives the spoils of war and the floats of
          conquered towns
Before his own car and wears triumphal laurel himself;
While, wreathed in wild bay, the soldiers shout, "All hail!"
          And chant, "Victory!"
Then may my friend Messalla show the crowds a touching sight
As he, the father, applauds the chariot passing by.

Grant this, Phoebus, so may your hair be ever unshorn,
So may your sister be chaste forever and ever.

II,6

_____

Macer has joined the army; what's to become of
          delicate Cupid?
Does he go along and pack weapons like a man on his back?
Though far campaigns take this man over land or shifting seas,
          Will he march beside him with a spear?
Boy-god, I beg you, brand this rebel who has left your bower.
Still better, call the deserter back to your ranks.
However, if you spare soldiers, here's one who'll be a
          soldier too,
Even the kind to fetch his water sloshing in his helmet.
I'm off to enlist, so goodbye Venus, goodbye girls!
The army's for me and the bugle call is joyful to me!

magna loquor, sed magnifice mihi magna locuto
    excutiunt clausae fortia verba fores.
iuravi quotiens rediturum ad limina nunquam!
    cum bene iuravi, pes tamen ipse redit.
acer Amor, fractas utinam tua tela sagittas
    si licet exstinctas aspiciamque faces!
tu miserum torques, tu me mihi dira precari
    cogis et insana mente nefanda loqui.
iam mala finissem leto, sed credula vitam
    Spes fovet et fore cras semper ait melius.

Spes alit agricolas, Spes sulcis credit aratis
    semina quae magno faenore reddat ager:
haec laqueo volucres, haec captat arundine pisces,
    cum tenues hamos abdidit ante cibus:
Spes etiam valida solatur compede vinctum:
    crura sonant ferro, sed canit inter opus:
Spes facilem Nemesim spondet mihi, sed negat illa:
    ei mihi, ne vincas, dura puella, deam.

parce, per immatura tuae precor ossa sororis:
    sic bene sub tenera parva quiescat humo.
illa mihi sancta est, illius dona sepulcro
    et madefacta meis serta feram lacrimis,
illius ad tumulum fugiam supplexque sedebo
    et mea cum muto fata querar cinere.
non feret usque suum te propter flere clientem:
    illius ut verbis, sis mihi lenta veto,
ne tibi neglecti mittant mala somnia manes,
    maestaque sopitae stet soror ante torum,
qualis ab excelsa praeceps delapsa fenestra
    venit ad infernos sanguinolenta lacus.

I talk big, yes, but after I've bragged my mightiest boast,
    A bolted door knocks the force from my words.
I swore I'd never go near that door again—
Swore up and down—yet my feet go right back by themselves.
    If possible, heartless Cupid, I'd wish
I could see your weapons, your arrows broken, your torch
    put out!
You torture me, a wretched man, you make me call
Dread curses upon myself and utter blasphemies insanely.
Long since, I'd have ended my woes in death, but
    credulous Hope
Warmed me to life by saying always tomorrow will be better.

    Hope! She sustains the farmer, Hope
Invests in the plowed-up furrows the seeds which the field
Returns with high interest. She catches birds in snares
And fish with rods when the bait has disguised the
    slender hook.
Hope comforts even the slave with fetters welded fast;
His shanks may clank with iron, but still he sings at his work.
Hope promises me a yielding Nemesis, but *she* refuses.
    Ah, stubborn girl, don't thwart this goddess!

Be kind, I beg by the bones of your sister too early dead,
So the child may sweetly sleep under soft-lying earth.
I hold her sacred; I'll bring gifts to her sepulchre,
    And wreaths all dripping with my tears.
I'll rush to her tomb and crouch there suppliant
    And moan my fate with her mute ashes.
She won't allow her protégé to weep for you forever.
As if in her words I protest, don't be unbending to me,
Lest that neglected spirit send you nightmares,
And in your sleep your lamented sister loom before your bed,
Looking as she did when, after falling headlong
From the high window, she went blood-covered to the
    rivers of Hades.

desino, no dominae luctus renoventur acerbi:
non ego sum tanti, ploret ut illa semel.

nec lacrimis oculos digna est foedare loquaces:
lena nocet nobis, ipsa puella bona est.
lena necat miserum Phryne furtimque tabellas
occulto portans itque reditque sinu:
saepe, ego cum dominae dulces a limine duro
agnosco voces, haec negat esse domi:
saepe, ubi nox promissa mihi est, languere puellam
nuntiat aut aliquas extimuisse minas.
tunc morior curis, tunc mens mihi perdita fingit,
quisve meam teneat, quot teneatve modis:
tunc tibi, lena, precor diras: satis anxia vivas,
moverit e votis pars quotacumque deos.

III, 19

Nulla tuum nobis subducet femina lectum:
hoc primum iuncta est foedere nostra Venus.
tu mihi sola places, nec iam te praeter in urbe
formosa est oculis ulla puella meis.
atque utinam posses uni mihi bella videri!
displiceas aliis: sic ego tutus ero.
nil opus invidia est, procul absit gloria vulgi:
qui sapit, in tacito gaudeat ille sinu.

I must leave off or I'll revive my girl's keen grief.
I'm not worth making her weep a single tear.

It isn't right for tears to spoil her speaking eyes.
That bawd! She's ruining us both! My girl is good in herself.
     The procuress, Phryne, is killing poor me,
Sneaking back and forth with love-notes hidden in her breast.
Often, though I recognize the sweet voice of my mistress
Beyond the hostile door, the hag tells me she's not at home.
And often, when the night's been promised me,
     She brings a message: my girl is sickly,
Or has been frightened by some threat. And I die
     from anguish;
My desperate brain envisions someone clasping my
     darling close
     And every position he holds her in.
Then I curse you, she-pimp, curse you! If any tiniest part
Of my prayers affects the gods, you'll live with trouble to spare.

III, 19

No woman shall steal your nest of love from me;
From the first our love was bound by such a vow.
You alone delight me, and still in all the city
No other girl but you is beautiful in my sight.
But oh that you might seem a beauty only to me!
May others find you ugly; thus, I'll be out of danger!
No need for envy; let me not adopt the rabble's boasting.
A wise man sings his joy in the closet of his heart.

sic ego secretis possum bene vivere silvis,
    qua nulla humano sit via trita pede.
tu mihi curarum requies, tu nocte vel atra
    lumen, et in solis tu mihi turba locis.
nunc licet e caelo mittatur amica Tibullo,
    mittetur frustra deficietque Venus.
hoc tibi sancta tuae Iunonis numina iuro,
    quae sola ante alios est mihi magna deos.

quid facio demens? heu heu mea pignora cedo.
    iuravi stulte: proderat iste timor.
nunc tu fortis eris, nunc tu me audacius ures:
    hoc peperit misero garrula lingua malum.
iam faciam quodcumque voles, tuus usque manebo,
    nec fugiam notae servitium dominae,
sed Veneris sanctae considam vinctus ad aras:
    haec notat iniustos supplicibusque favet.

III, 20

Rumor ait crebro nostram peccare puellam:
    nunc ego me surdis auribus esse velim.
crimina non haec sunt nostro sine facta dolore:
    quid miserum torques, rumor acerbe? tace.

In this way I could live happily in solitary woods
Where human feet have never beaten a path.
For me you are a balm for cares, a light in blackest night,
    And in lonely deserts my teeming world.
Now even if from heaven itself a mistress were sent Tibullus,
She'd come in vain, for passion's fire would fail.
This, by Juno's sacred majesty, I swear to you,
And she alone is greater to me than any other deity.

How crazy! What am I doing? Good heavens, I'm giving up
My mortgage on you. I vowed like a dunce! Your fear itself
Would help me. Now you'll be strong and with more boldness
    burn me.
My babbling tongue has done this mischief to me, poor thing.
Now, whatever you may do, I'll still be yours forever.
I'll not flee bondage to my acknowledged mistress,
But settle down in chains by the altar of holy Venus,
Who brands renegades and gives her suppliants aid.

III, 20

Gossip says my girl is often deceiving me.
I wish my ears were straightway struck stone deaf.
These charges aren't flung out without causing pain to me.
Why torture wretched victims, gallish Gossip? Shut up!

NO
HARM
TO LOVERS

The Love of Sulpicia and Cerinthus
As Revealed in Six Elegies
by Sulpicia
and
Five Elegies
by Tibullus

A PREFATORY NOTE

One member of Messalla's household was Sulpicia, the daughter of Servius Sulpicius and, very likely, Messalla's sister Valeria. Servius is thought to have been dead at this time, and thus Messalla had become Sulpicia's guardian. The girl was of an ancient, aristocratic family, was said to have been beautiful, and was certainly adept at keeping pace with the intellectual, rather unconventional, company about her. Though it may seem natural, from her association with so many poets, that she should begin to write poetry, it is strange that only six brief and very personal poems have come down to us, all concerned with the difficulties of her love for the young man, Cerinthus, and that she never, so far as we know, wrote any more poetry. Except for a few fragments by other ladies, these six poems make up the extant body of classical Latin poetry by women.

Sulpicia's poems were not written to be artistic creations, as were those of Tibullus which are based on them; the only artfulness about hers is that she expressed her emotion in verses rather than in prose or in speech to the man concerned. "With the exception of the first,* which reads like an entry in her diary," wrote Kirby Flower Smith, "these pieces are in the

* This appears as her last poem in my arrangement of her work.

form of brief notes addressed to Cerinthus himself, and it seems evident that none of them was ever intended for publication." One may ask why she bothered with meter at all; and then one should realize that her love for Cerinthus was a very delicate, rather secret and, judging from his attitude, by no means reassuring matter. Her mother, Valeria, was watching her and planning a "proper match," though Cerinthus was apparently a presentable young man, at least gentleman enough to go hunting, which was a prerogative of the upper classes at that time. And her uncle, Messalla, even though Cerinthus was frequently in his house, seemed totally unaware of Sulpicia's interests and probably thought a nice rest in the country would calm her fidgety ways. The worst of it all was that Cerinthus was a very shy young man, not even, according to Sulpicia (via Tibullus), able to speak his intimate prayers aloud, a mandatory act if the prayers were to be answered. In her first two notes to him, she had to suggest, and in no uncertain terms, the bent of her mind.

For myself, I like to believe that Tibullus wrote the elegies about her love affair, though it can be neither proved nor disproved. The weight of evidence suggests that he did; and certainly they were written by someone of Messalla's circle. But more than that, I like to believe that Tibullus helped Sulpicia to write poetry, that he was her confidant, and that her confessions revealed to him the actual flesh—as opposed to the inherited, traditional artifices—of the classical elegy. I like to think that he wrote these five poems just for her, as encouragement to her spirit to persist, since he so often speaks for taciturn Cerinthus; and that, when the happy culmination was reached (after the event of the final poem, I picture a formal marriage), she put away Tibullus's verses with her own in a chest—a "memory" chest.

If she did marry the young man, perhaps their life together was too full of happiness for her to think of writing more; certainly the poems we have spring from a longing unfulfilled, yet still with a strong hopefulness behind it. But perhaps marriage was the door to deep sorrow, a despair to which her modest talent could not, had not the heart to, give expression. At any rate, this romancing embroidery on the edges of the work which is left could account for the fact that the Tibullus poems were not published until many years later, unauthenticated but adjoined to his other work, and with them were the Sulpicia poems.

But whatever fortune the marriage may have brought her, the culmination of her love affair in marriage cries out for an epithalamium from Tibullus, who watched it with such interest. It is more than likely that the birthday poem for Cornutus (II, 2) is this poem. Cornutus could have been the actual man who was veiled under the name of Cerinthus, just as Catullus's Clodia was veiled as Lesbia. The parallel of some of the lines with the Cerinthus poems is a possible additional clue, though the imagery is a common elegiac device. But most of all, the character of Cornutus is the same as that of Cerinthus, the tongue-tied man who cannot speak even his wish to his Birth Genius; so that, whether Cornutus or Cerinthus, his prayers must still be phrased by Tibullus and, in his birthday poem, provide the happy ending to an ancient love-affair.

Acting upon Kirby Flower Smith's remarks that the poems have always been printed in a sequence which is neither chronological nor psychological, I have rearranged Sulpicia's poems according to the more reasonable progression he suggested. And I have tried to match them with the Tibullus poems apparently based upon hers, so that in reading one moves through a record of intimate fragments and comments on her love: early longing, bewilderment, hesitation, hurt, jealous scorn and final triumph. All the titles are obviously my own additions and are not in the original manuscripts or editions.

TIBULLUS
III,8

Sulpicia est tibi culta tuis, Mars magne, kalendis:
    spectatum e caelo, si sapis, ipse veni.
hoc Venus ignoscet: at tu, violente, caveto
    ne tibi miranti turpiter arma cadant.
illius ex oculis, cum vult exurere divos,
    accendit geminas lampadas acer Amor.
illam, quidquid agit, quoquo vestigia movit,
    componit furtim subsequiturque Decor.
seu solvit crines, fusis decet esse capillis:
    seu compsit, comptis est veneranda comis.
urit, seu Tyria voluit procedere palla:
    urit, seu nivea candida veste venit.
talis in aeterno felix Vertumnus Olympo
    mille habet ornatus, mille decenter habet.

sola puellarum digna est cui mollia caris
    vellera det sucis bis madefacta Tyros,
possideatque metit quidquid bene olentibus arvis
    cultor odoratae dives Arabs segetis
et quascumque niger rubro de litore gemmas
    proximus Eois colligit Indus aquis.

hanc vos, Pierides, festis cantate kalendis,
    et testudinea Phoebe superbe lyra.
hoc sollemne sacrum multos haec sumet in annos:
    dignior est vestro nulla puella choro.

TIBULLUS:
The Matronalia, March 1

Sulpicia is adorned for you on your high day, great Mars.
Come, if you're wise, from heaven and see for yourself.
Venus will overlook it. But be careful, hothead,
Not to let your armor shamefully fall while you marvel.
    When prickly Love would sting the gods
    He lights twin torches from her eyes.
Whatever she does, wherever she turns a footstep,
Grace invisibly trails behind and sees that all is proper.
If she loosens her hair, it's becoming to wear streaming hair;
If she binds it up, she must be worshiped for braided tresses.
She lights desire if she chooses to stroll in a Tyrian gown,
Desire, if she comes in a mist of snowy clothes.
On eternal Olympus, fertile Vertumnus, like her
Has a thousand costumes and wears them all with grace.

She alone of maidens is worthy for Tyre to send her
    Soft wool double-dyed with precious juice,
And to have what the rich Arabian, farming fragrant soil,
    Reaps with skill from his musky fields,
And all the pearls the swarthy Indian gathers
    From crimson shores near the tides of Dawn.

Pierian maidens, sing of her on this holiday Kalends;
And Phoebus, sing, proud of your tortoise lyre.
This solemn feast will she hold for many years to come.
    No girl is more worthy for your band.

SULPICIA
III, 14

Invisus natalis adest qui rure molesto
et sine Cerintho tristis agendus erit.
dulcius urbe quid est? an villa sit apta puellae
atque Arretino frigidus amnis agro?
iam, nimium Messalla mei studiose, quiescas,
neu tempestivae saepe propinque viae.
hic animum sensusque meos abducta relinquo,
arbitrio quamvis non sinis esse meo.

SULPICIA
III, 15

Scis iter ex animo sublatum triste puellae?
natali Romae iam licet esse meo.
omnibus ille dies nobis natalis agatur,
qui nec opinanti nunc tibi forte venit.

SULPICIA:
To Cerinthus—1

My hated birthday's coming, which will have to be spent
Gloomily in the irksome country, and without Cerinthus.
    What's more fun than the city?
Are farmhouse or frigid stream in Arretium's fields
    A proper place for a girl?
Messalla, you're too solicitous of me. Relax now.
Excursions, Uncle, sometimes aren't quite convenient.
You may drag me away, but here I leave my heart and soul,
Though you deny me them for my own disposal.

SULPICIA:
Later, to Cerinthus

You know the weight of that dreary trip is removed
From your sweetheart's mind? Now I can have my birthday
    here in Rome.
Let's all celebrate this occasion, which comes
As a chance, perhaps a bit surprising now, for you.

TIBULLUS
III, 12

Natalis Iuno, sanctos cape turis acervos
   quos tibi dat tenera docta puella manu.
tota tibi est hodie, tibi se laetissima compsit,
   staret ut ante tuos conspicienda focos.
illa quidem ornandi causas tibi, diva, relegat:
   est tamen occulte cui placuisse velit.

at tu, sancta, fave, neu quis divellat amantes,
   sed iuveni quaeso mutua vincla para.
sic bene compones: ullae non ille puellae
   servire aut cuiquam dignior illa viro.
nec possit cupidos vigilans deprendere custos,
   fallendique vias mille ministret Amor.
adnue purpureaque veni perlucida palla:
   ter tibi fit libo, ter, dea casta, mero.
praecipit et natae mater studiosa quod optet:
   illa aliud tacita, iam sua, mente rogat.
uritur, ut celeres urunt altaria flammae,
   nec, liceat quamvis, sana fuisse velit.

sis iuveni grata, et veniet cum proximus annus,
   hic idem votis iam vetus adsit amor.

TIBULLUS:

Intercession, on Sulpicia's birthday,
addressed to her Guardian Spirit

Accept the holy mounds of incense, Birthday Juno,
Offered you by the gentle hands of this accomplished girl.
     She dedicates this whole day to you.
She is attired most richly to stand, admired by all,
Before your altar. She even puts the blame on you, O goddess,
     For her adornment. But secretly
There's a certain someone she would like to please.

So Heavenly One, be kind; let no one part these lovers,
But link her with the youth in mutual bonds, I beg.
     You would do well to join them so:
For him, no girl more worthy to serve for love; for her,
     no man;
Let the prying chaperon be unable to catch them in
     their passions,
And let Love provide a thousand ways to baffle.
Agree, and come in your light-filled purple robes.
Three gifts of wine and three of cake are offered you,
     holy goddess,
And the zealous mother guides the prayer her child must make.
     But the daughter, now self-assured,
Prays a different one within her silent heart.
She burns as quick licking flames burn on the altar,
And even though she could be, would not wish to be healed.

Indulge the youth, and when the next year comes round
     Let this love, already long enduring,
          Through their prayers remain the same.

SULPICIA
III, 17

Estne tibi, Cerinthe, tuae pia cura puellae,
    quod mea nunc vexat corpora fessa calor?
a ego non aliter tristes evincere morbos
    optarim, quam te si quoque velle putem.
at mihi quid prosit morbos evincere, si tu
    nostra potes lento pectore ferre mala?

TIBULLUS
III, 10

Huc ades et tenerae morbos expelle puellae,
    huc ades, intonsa Phoebe superbe coma.
crede mihi, propera: nec te iam, Phoebe, pigebit
    formosae medicas applicuisse manus.
effice ne macies pallentes occupet artus,
    neu notet informis pallida membra color,
et quodcumque mali est et quidquid triste timemus,
    in pelagus rapidis evehat amnis aquis.
sancte, veni, tecumque feras quicumque sapores,
    quicumque et cantus corpora fessa levant:

SULPICIA:
Chiding Cerinthus

Have you no tender thoughts, Cerinthus, for your girl,
Now when fever shivers my feeble body?
Ah, I'd never hope to conquer bleak disease
    Unless I thought you desired it too.
For what good for me to triumph over sickness, if you
    Can face my woes with indifferent heart?

TIBULLUS:
Plea and counsel

Come here and exorcise the illness of this lovely girl.
Come here, Phoebus, proud in your uncropped hair.
Believe me, hurry! You won't soon regret, Phoebus,
Applying to her beauty the medicine of your hands.
See that no blight invades her feeble members,
No morbid color blotches her pallid limbs.
And all the ills and corruption that we dread,
    Let surging streams discharge in the sea.
Come, holy one, and bring whatever medicines
Or incantations relieve the ailing body.

neu iuvenem torque metuit qui fata puellae
    votaque pro domina vix numeranda facit.
interdum vovet, interdum, quod langueat illa,
    dicit in aeternos aspera verba deos.

pone metum, Cerinthe: deus non laedit amantes.
    tu modo semper ama: salva puella tibi est.
nil opus est fletu: lacrimis erit aptius uti,
    si quando fuerit tristior illa tibi.
at nunc tota tua est, te solum candida secum
    cogitat, et frustra credula turba sedet.

Phoebe, fave: laus magna tibi tribuetur in uno
    corpore servato restituisse duos.
iam celeber, iam laetus eris, cum debita reddet
    certatim sanctis laetus uterque focis.
tunc te felicem dicet pia turba deorum,
    optabunt artes et sibi quisque tuas.

SULPICIA

III, 18

Ne tibi sim, mea lux, aeque iam fervida cura
    ac videor paucos ante fuisse dies,
si quicquam tota commisi stulta iuventa
    cuius me fatear paenituisse magis,
hesterna quam te solum quod nocte reliqui,
    ardorem cupiens dissimulare meum.

Don't plague this youth who fears for his sweetheart's life
    And pledges countless vows to save her.
At times he prays; at times, because she languishes,
He hurls rough words against the eternal gods.

Cast out your fear, Cerinthus. God does no harm to lovers.
Just love her always and your girl is safe.
No need to weep. Tears will be more in keeping
If ever she starts to doubt you. But now she's all your own;
The fair girl thinks of no one but you alongside her,
And a credulous crowd is waiting for her in vain.

Phoebus, give them your aid. You'll garner lofty praise
    For restoring two lives by saving one.
Then you'll be famous, joyful then, when the happy pair
Eagerly vie to pay their debt to your holy altar.
Then the righteous host of gods will call you fortunate
And each will covet for himself your mighty arts.

SULPICIA:
To Cerinthus—2

My love-light, may I be no more a fire so glowing
To your love as I feel I was some days ago,
If I, in all my callow years, did any stupid act
For which I would confess more keen regret
    Than running out on you last night,
Leaving you alone, because I longed to cover my burning love.

TIBULLUS
III,11

Qui mihi te, Cerinthe, dies dedit, hic mihi sanctus
    atque inter festos semper habendus erit.
te nascente novum Parcae cecinere puellis
    servitium et dederunt regna superba tibi.
uror ego ante alias: iuvat hoc, Cerinthe, quod uror,
    si tibi de nobis mutuus ignis adest.
mutuus adsit amor, per te dulcissima furta
    perque tuos oculos per Geniumque rogo.

mane Geni, cape tura libens votisque faveto,
    si modo, cum de me cogitat, ille calet.
quod si forte alios iam nunc suspiret amores,
    tunc precor infidos, sancte, relinque focos.

nec tu sis iniusta, Venus: vel serviat aeque
    vinctus uterque tibi, vel mea vincla leva.
sed potius valida teneamur uterque catena,
    nulla queat posthac nos soluisse dies.

optat idem iuvenis quod nos, sed tectius optat:
    nam pudet haec illum dicere verba palam.
at tu, Natalis, quoniam deus omnia sentis,
    adnue: quid refert clamne palamne roget?

TIBULLUS:

He speaks for the girl,
on Cerinthus' birthday

This day, Cerinthus, which gave you to the world for me,
Shall ever be sacred to me, to be placed among the festivals.
    When you were born, the Fates predicted
New thralldom for girls and gave proud dominion over them
    to you.
More than all others I burn for you. I rejoice in burning,
Cerinthus, if equal fire, kindled by mine, is flaming in you.
By your Birth Spirit, by your eyes, by sweetest stolen ardors,
    May your love match with mine, I pray.

Kind Spirit, please accept incense and grant my prayer:
Just that, when he thinks of me, he may flush with passion;
But if by chance he should be sighing even now
    For some other love, O holy one,
Then I beg you, forsake his faithless fireside altar.

And you, Venus, be not unjust. Make both of us your slaves
In equal bondage, or strike my chains away.
But rather let each of us hold the other fast
With mighty chains that no hereafter can dissolve from us.

The young man's longings mirror mine, but he longs
    more covertly,
For he's ashamed to speak his prayer-words aloud.
So then, Birth Spirit, god who knows all things, promise!
What matter if he plead aloud or mute?

SULPICIA
III, 16

Gratum est, securus multum quod iam tibi de me
　permittis, subito ne male inepta cadam.
sit tibi cura togae potior pressumque quasillo
　scortum quam Servi filia Sulpicia.
solliciti sunt pro nobis, quibus illa dolori est
　ne cedam ignoto, maxima causa, toro.

TIBULLUS
III, 9

Parce meo iuveni, seu quis bona pascua campi
　seu colis umbrosi devia montis aper,
nec tibi sit duros acuisse in proelia dentes:
　incolumem custos hunc mihi servet Amor.
sed procul abducit venandi Delia cura:
　o pereant silvae deficiantque canes!
quis furor est, quae mens, densos indagine colles
　claudentem teneras laedere velle manus?

SULPICIA:
To Cerinthus—3

I must really thank you that, sure of me now, you assume so
  much license,
Lest I, a nitwit, suddenly take a tumble into evil.
Chasing a skirt, a pickup packing a basket of wool,
May concern you more than does Sulpicia, daughter of Servius.
But some are anxious for me; their greatest cause for worry
Is that I may lose to a pallet of dirty love.

TIBULLUS:
Cerinthus forgiven;
once more Tibullus speaks for the girl

Spare my sweetheart, boar, whether you dwell in grass-
  green meadows
Or in thickets of distant darkling mountains.
Don't think of whetting your cruel tusks for a fight.
Let his guardian, Cupid, bring him safe and sound to me.
But the Delian Lady lures him with love of hunting.
If only the forests would shrivel and hounds die out!
What madness is this, what reason in it, to hurt those

quidve iuvat furtim latebras intrare ferarum
candidaque hamatis crura notare rubis?

sed tamen, ut tecum liceat, Cerinthe, vagari,
    ipsa ego per montes retia torta feram,
ipsa ego velocis quaeram vestigia cervi
    et demam celeri ferrea vincla cani.
tunc mihi, tunc placeant silvae, si, lux mea, tecum
    arguar ante ipsas concubuisse plagas:
tunc veniat licet ad casses, inlaesus abibit,
    ne Veneris cupidae gaudia turbet, aper.

nunc sine me sit nulla Venus, sed lege Dianae,
    caste puer, casta retia tange manu:
et quaecumque meo furtim subrepit amori,
    incidat in saevas diripienda feras.

at tu venandi studium concede parenti,
    et celer in nostros ipse recurre sinus.

tender hands
In locking a cordon round the thick-tangled slopes?
Or what delight, to enter stealthily into the coverts
Of savage game and scratch white shins on bramble-thorns?

And yet if I may range with you, Cerinthus,
I myself will pack the intricate nets across the scarps
    And trail the spoor of the darting deer,
Unleash the iron collar of the leaping hound.
Then I'd like the woods, my sweet, then, if it's proved
That in the very snares, with love you pierced me,
    your quarry.
Then, though the boar approach the nets, he will
    leave unhurt
To keep from breaking the rapture of our passionate love.

Let there now be no love without me; but under Diana's law,
Innocent boy, touch the nets with innocent hands.
And may any slinking female who would decoy my lover
Chance among raging beasts and be torn to ribbons!

So yield your zeal for hunting to your elders
    And run back quickly into my arms.

SULPICIA
III, 13

Tandem venit amor, qualem texisse pudori
    quam nudasse alicui sit mihi fama magis.
exorata meis illum Cytherea Camenis
    attulit in nostrum deposuitque sinum.
exsolvit promissa Venus: mea gaudia narret,
    dicetur si quis non habuisse sua.
non ego signatis quicquam mandare tabellis,
    ne legat id nemo quam meus ante, velim,
sed peccasse iuvat, vultus componere famae
    taedet: cum digno digna fuisse ferar.

SULPICIA:
To Cerinthus—4

At last comes such a love that I'd be more ashamed
If gossip said I concealed it, than if I told someone.
The Cytherean, persuaded by my poetry's plea,
Has brought him here and wrapped him in my arms.
    Venus has kept her promise.
Let people tell my joy who never, it's said, found their own.
I wish I didn't have to seal any letter to my lover
Just to keep someone else from reading it first,
But I'm glad of my guilt and hate to calm my features
    for gossip.
Let's tell that it happened—a fitting, a fair exchange.

NOTES
TO THE POEMS

These notes to Tibullus's elegies include specific remarks on each separate poem but exclude identification of proper names, which may be found in the glossary. Some of the relevant cross-references to other elegies are given in parentheses, but, since there are no line references, these instances may be tedious to locate and should therefore be ignored by all but the insatiably curious who wish to pursue a topic through every occurrence. References and quotations from Kirby Flower Smith's edition of The Elegies of Albius Tibullus *are indicated by "KFS."*

I,1

The first of five elegies dealing with Tibullus's love for Delia. It is quite likely that this was not her real name, since it was usual for poets to give pseudonyms to sweethearts in their poems (Catullus's Lesbia was really Clodia, and Propertius's Cynthia was Hostia). Delia's real name may have been Plania, as Apuleius suggested, some two hundred years after her time. At any rate, Delia, as an epithet of the goddess Diana (born at Delos) and sister of Apollo, god of poetry and song, was a suitable name for a poet's beloved. Her social status was probably that of a freedwoman (if not by birth at least under the law), and of a kept woman who eventually did not restrict her favors to the man who paid the bills. However, in this first elegy, she is not so much the ordinary courtesan she was to become, as a pleasant mistress who might even be considered a prospect for marriage.

In 42 B.C. Octavianus, under pressure, had confiscated large landholdings of rich men in favor of the veterans of the battle of Philippi. The family of Tibullus, like that of Vergil and of Propertius, was among those who suffered a reduction of income as a result.

The superstitions about crossways, so prevalent in ancient times, have endured to some extent to the present, as shown by the frequency of Christian shrines at such locations.

As a sacrifice, the lamb, rather than the heifer, was more indicative of a poor man.

Dog days, of course, take their name from the Dog Star, Sirius, which was supposed to have a definite influence on the intense heat of mid-summer.

As everyone knows, the gods do not object to "humble gifts," not even our own "widow's mite." Cleanliness, as of the earthen bowls, was a requisite in worship of the gods.

The south wind (Auster) which brought storms was often spoken of as cold and, in personification, it poured out the rain which followed it. In its Greek counterpart, Notos, it is shown on the Temple of the Winds at Athens, pouring from an urn.

Messalla, Tibullus's patron and friend, was of a distinguished family and served as commander at Philippi. After the death of Brutus and Cassius and the defeat of the army, the soldiers chose him as their general. Later he served with Anthony but left him for Octavianus for whom he fought in Sicily, at Actium and in Aquitania (I, 7). War trophies belonged to the family of the conqueror (as long as it kept the house in its possession) and were displayed in the vestibule of the house (the portico) which, in the case of a rich man like Messalla, was no doubt quite large.

The doorkeeper, or janitor, was a slave and was chained to the doorpost.

Mourning for the dead involved sufficient but not immoderate tribute. All will weep, and hence there is no need for hiring mourners, a custom which has prevailed to our own times. It was usual to unbind the hair, and the bereft, if deeply grieved, pulled it out or cut it off, and also scratched his face. In this instance, such gestures, though showing satisfying lamentation, would destroy Delia's beauty.

Lovers, for one or another reason, were often locked out; and lovers' quarrels, involving violence to the person and the house, were fairly commonplace both as a literary theme and as a conventional phase in love-making.

I,2

The second of the five elegies about Delia. KFS suggests that the setting is a Roman supper room where several friends of the poet are gathered.

The Romans by custom drank wine mixed with water in regulated proportions. *"Merum,"* the word used for wine in the first line, is straight, or neat, wine, by analogy with the adjective "unmixed."

Roman doors swung, not on hinges, but on pivots set in sockets in the threshold and the lintel. KFS cites the Elizabethan Tourneur's description of a cunning woman who nailed leather hinges to her door to avoid its telltale squeaks. The doors were bolted by bars, rather than by locks, and opened outward so that the outside bar could not be removed by those inside the house without a key. The janitor frequently held the key. Delia would have to throw the bar with an inserted prong or stick, such as we today use to lift a hook or latch on some doors, when we are on the wrong side.

The Roman lover wore garlands about his head when he went to call and hung them on the door as a calling card when his sweetheart was not at home.

Venus here assumes the function of Fortune in the proverb "Fortune favors the brave," thus transforming it for the erotic purposes of elegy.

It was a prevalent idea that the divine powers (Venus in this case) looked out for poets, prophets, madmen and lovers (II, 5; III, 10); today this providence is extended to drunkards.

The allusion to Venus's "birthright of blood and furious seas" as the origin of her fierceness when her intentions are crossed goes back to her Grecian counterpart, Aphrodite ("foam-born"). In the Homeric version she was the daughter of Zeus and Dione. Tibullus refers to another legend: Saturn, a Titan, had been cast into the infernal regions by his father Uranus, but at the instigation of his mother Gaea he rebelled, castrated his father and flung his penis into the sea. Foam gathered about the bleeding flesh and from it Aphrodite was born.

The "witch" is the *saga* or more specifically the *lena,* a procuress who arranged love affairs and was adept in magic and love potions. The powers mentioned are the conventional ones associated with such women. Bones of the dead are useful charms, even today, for conjure and hoodoo women. Ghosts, summoned from Hades by necromancy, would never return unless placated by offerings of milk. The idea that wizards could influence the weather was almost universal.

Belief in the supernatural power of three is worldwide. Spitting was to avert harm and insure protection; it recurs later in this elegy with the suggestion of "God forbid that I. . . ."

The effect of the charm is that it will work only for Tibullus; Delia's master will see any other men who make love to her. Behind the allusion is belief in the magical properties and susceptibilities of names: merely by knowing one's name a witch can work a charm. In some primitive tribes the true name is carefully concealed from untrusted outsiders by each individual.

The soldier who forsakes love for war and plunder is not only a crass man to whom greed is more important than idyllic love, but a rich man who easily becomes the poet's rival—both conventional elegiac figures (I, 5; II, 3). "Cilician troops" is possibly a reference to Messalla's expedition mentioned in I, 7.

Garlands were not stolen from the temples because of wanton sacrilege, but because poverty prohibited the buying of flowers to give a mistress. Falling prostrate at the altar and kissing it, crawling and beating the head against the pillars, all suggest medieval Christian penances. To Romans they suggested the worship of Isis.

The man who mocks young lovers will come face to face with the laws of retribution, justice and fate, here put into effect by Cupid. It suggests the caprice of the Wheel of Fortune and our phrase, "a long road that has no turning."

I,3

The third of the five elegies about Delia.

Messalla was sent, presumably soon after the battle of Actium (31 B.C.), to the Orient by Octavianus to deal with disturbed conditions there. Tibullus was invited to go along, as was customary in the case of literary men. (Messalla appears in Shakespeare's *Julius Caesar;* also a poet [Act IV, Scene 3, in Brutus's tent in the army camp] of whom Brutus says, "What should the wars do with these jigging fools?")

Corcyra, the land of the Phaeacians in Homer, is known today as Corfu, an island in the Ionian Sea off the north coast of Greece.

Though most perfumes came from Arabia, they were generally spoken of as Syrian because they were shipped from Syrian ports.

Fortune-telling by drawing sacred lots, classified as *"sortes,"* was similar to the contemporary use of cards. The lots were small tabs, often of wood, inscribed with vague statements and were drawn out of an urn in which they were mixed together. The drawing was usually done for the curious client by a small boy and then interpreted by the *sortilegus,* or fortune reader. Children, as all know, are proper for such actions and are still used in lotteries, raffles, etc. Delia draws three lots because the number is mystic and lucky. It is odd, however, that *she* drew them rather than the boy, and that the boy interpreted, rather than a sortilegus. The latter operated not only in the temples, particularly that of Fortuna at Praeneste, but also in the streets and busy sections of cities.

Birds always gave good and bad signs when alive, just as when dead they showed in their entrails, by divination, omens. In Tibullus's time other animals were also used.

The mention here of "Saturn's day" is, according to KFS, the earliest surviving reference in Latin literature to what has become known to us as Saturday. It was considered an unlucky day, though many looked on that attitude as a foreign superstition, because of the original connection with the Sabbath of the Jews who had begun to come into Rome after Pompey's conquests (63 B.C.).

Stumbling is always a bad omen, especially when it happens at the threshold; for this reason brides are carried into their new home, just as the Romans used to do.

Though Delia observed the rites of Isis, she had not managed to dispel the curse Tibullus brought on himself by disdaining the will of Venus.

Sistra were metal rattles which were an inseparable part of the worship of Isis. They were used in the regular morning and evening services and in the periods of prayer and meditation in the temple. Priests of Isis had shaven heads, but women serving her wore their hair loose, as was usual in most rites, whether for the dead or for magical purposes or any worship.

The fact that no house had doors suggested a lost state of bliss, such as the Golden Age just described, for now a girl can shut her door in the face of a lover—a frequent occurrence to Tibullus as well as other elegists.

According to popular belief, honey was the food of the gods and fell as their gift to man in a dew which had a special tendency to settle on oak trees.

The products of the Age of Iron (for Tibullus, his contemporary age) ruled over by Jove—war, armies and swords—are developed in a later treatment of the Golden Age, as causes of man's woes and his fall from a state of bliss (I, 10). Wars and ships, the instruments by which merchants and soldiers fed their greed (I, 2; II, 3) and promoted it in others, were temptations to "untimely death" because they violated the laws of nature and the gods. The bliss of the Golden Age, however, was often a subject for comedy and satire: rivers of wine (as in the heaven of some early Christian writers) ; rivers of hot soup with gobs of floating meat; roast pigs that ran about asking to be eaten. The most recent analogy to the last is the "Schmoo" in Al Capp's comic strip, "Li'l Abner."

Epitaphs and votive inscriptions were characteristic motives of elegy (I, 9).

The customary conductor of departed souls to the other world was Mercury, but Tibullus, because of his especial devotion to love, will be brought by Venus to the Elysian Fields. In this paradise, each gains what he was denied on earth, and so those who died for love are rewarded with endless happy love and wreathed with the myrtle sacred to Venus.

The "abode of the wicked" (the wicked here are obviously any persons who had harmed Tibullus and his love) is Tartarus, originally the prison of the Titans and indescribably deep and black. The rivers surrounding it are Cocytus, flowing with howls of lamentation and tears, and Phlegethon, flowing with stormy black fires.

The offending part of Tityos' body is punished, as was customary. The Latin word would mean generally viscera or bowels, but because of the crime, it would connote the liver, which was considered the seat of passion. Today we should say the "heart."

The punishment of the daughters of Danaus for offending the will of Venus derives from several superstitions relating to rituals, marriage and unmarried women: as perjurers of marriage vows, they must forever try to fill a bottomless bath, bathing being a regular part of wedding ceremonials.

The loose hair and naked feet of Delia do not imply untidiness; they were customary for women in the home.

I,4

The first of three elegies involving the boy Marathus, who apparently belonged to Tibullus. It is mainly a mock didactic "art of love" (homosexual division) and does not suggest, until the last few lines, that Tibullus may really have had erotic feelings toward the boy.

The advice of Priapus, who was never noted as well-bred, eloquent, dignified or learned, takes on conventional characteristics of a pedantic system and by exaggeration lends irony and comedy to his instructions.

The "tender gangs of boys" would have the typical attractions of the effeminate boy (*puer delicatus*): innocence, shyness, absence of a beard and paleness.

Perjuries of love pledges were declared unpunishable by Jove when, after he had sworn fidelity to his wife Juno, she surprised him making love to Io.

Diana and Minerva, both confirmed virgins, would have the least sympathy of any deities for lovers and their wrongdoings; but even they would not punish broken vows of love.

Neither Bacchus nor Phoebus Apollo could ever grow old and both had long uncut hair, since boys' hair was not cut until their majority.

The slave of love would of course offer to carry the hunting snares (III, 9).

The identity and purpose of Titius is uncertain. Possibly he was a young poet, friend of Horace (Epistle I, 3, 9), who accompanied Tiberius to Asia in 20 B.C. He is probably used to give a sharp turn at the end of the poem: Tibullus has been inquiring of Priapus not for himself but for his friend, only to reveal that he himself really wants the requested aid, and can now become a "professor in love." But even so, his instructions fail him.

No poet following Tibullus has mentioned Marathus, and many scholars have assumed that he was not a real person but an imaginary one on whom to hang a conventional elegy on the theme of homosexual love, imitated from Greek models. The fact remains that the same actual basis for such poems continued among the Romans, growing more flagrant after Tibullus's time, and that absence of reference by later writers does not mean that such persons did not exist.

I,5

The fourth of the five elegies about Delia.

Punishment visited on the unruly, rebellious or scornful by the powers of Fate and Retribution was usual; here it falls upon the boastful.

As a practical disinfectant sulphur was held in high esteem by both Greeks and Romans for purifying powers and sorcery. Disease was considered a demon to be exorcised by these methods. The evil dreams suggest delirium caused by malarial fevers so common in Rome, with its adjacent swamps and mosquitoes (III, 10; III, 17). There is, however, a connection between bad dreams and the goddess Trivia (Hecate), who sends all sorts of lunacy on people and is associated with Luna and Diana, and in addition, the widespread belief in the influence of the moon on disease.

The holy meal in offerings was a salted meal and was used in all sacrifices. Priests traditionally covered their heads in rites, and usually any others involved did so, too.

Three and, its multiple, nine were often associated with worship of Trivia and her alias Hecate.

The "wild winds" are, in the Latin text, Eurus, the southeast or east wind, and Notus, the south wind. These winds obviously could never blow anything from Rome to Armenia, the land of perfumes in this poem (though Syria is usually the place mentioned).

Of the lover's wine turning to tears, KFS says: "I have found no parallel for this pretty conceit." A recent hillbilly song is called "Just pour me a glass of tear-drops."

Thetis's magical ability to change shapes (she became a bird, a tree, a tiger) to escape Peleus's advances relates to Delia's shifts to avoid the poet.

Blood and gall, when drunk, were presumed to drive a person mad. The owl was the worst omen of evil the Romans could picture, and its lighting upon a roof multiplied its menace. Witches were supposed to turn into screech-owls in Roman times (into cats or black dogs or wolves in medieval times); there was a natural connection with bats and vampirism. To eat grass or other plants from graves would invite punishment for sacrilege; and the plants, having magic powers from their location, could take their own revenge. Wolves were always imbued with magical properties and characteristics; and, by the principle of magic association, eating anything which wolves had mouthed was to invoke the nature of wolves. Hence the bawd is stricken with wolf-madness, lycanthropy, and even the dogs sacred to Hecate of the Crossroads sense that she is a werewolf and is probably after the food-offerings to Hecate.

Roman stag suppers were frequently attended by women of Delia's type and class. Their presence, like that of strip-tease girls today, did not destroy the stag nature of the party. Sandals were always removed at dinners, but usually they were drawn off by a slave—here, Tibullus, the slave of love.

To clear the throat and spit was a common twin-method of attracting attention; for some centuries now, it has given way to the delicate cough.

I,6

The last of the five elegies about Delia.

Cupid, the god of love, in earlier times had been a god to be feared, but by the era of Tibullus he had been modified into the

Alexandrian type of a spoiled, mischievous boy. Upbraiding the gods for belittling themselves by easy conquests over helpless mankind was fairly common in both Greek and Roman poetry. Compare the opening of this elegy with the middle section of I, 8, addressed to an experienced woman.

Ample togas which undulated in a flamboyant way were an affectation of exquisites, fops and dandies (I, 8; II, 3).

Women like Delia found the rites of Bellona (see Glossary) pleasing in the hysteric ceremonies such as the priestess here follows. Though the service seems to relate to war, the prophecy trivially concerns a war of love.

The fillet (*vitta*) and the long gown (*stola*) were reserved exclusively for virtuous married women of rank (*matronae*) and could not be worn by slaves, freedwomen, foreign women and prostitutes. This reference, which establishes Delia's social position, indicates that she belonged, most likely, to the class of freedwomen (*libertinae*).

I,7

When the natives of Aquitania rebelled, Messalla was sent to subdue them, and on his return from the successful expedition he was given a triumph on September 25, 27 B.C. Since his birthday fell shortly after this date, Tibullus celebrated it in this poem which makes his patron a man of destiny in civic and military affairs.

A triumph was a religious observation as well as a military pageant and was the final act in fulfilment of vows made to Capitoline Jove by the noble commander. KFS: ". . . until his return to the Capitol he was actually the representative of the Capitoline Jove. The procession was formed outside the city as a rule and entered by the Porta Triumphalis on the borders of the Campus Martius. Here it was met by the senate and citizens and proceeded to the Capitol, which was the goal of the ceremony. The procession was headed by the senate and officials of the state, then came the musicians and after them a long line—as long as possible—of spoils taken from the enemy, allegorical floats, distinguished captives in chains, etc., then the soldiers roaring out ribald songs upon their general to protect him from the evil eye in this hour of his dangerously good fortune, and finally the triumphator himself with all the insignia of his divine prototype on the Capitol, in a chariot of gold and ivory drawn by four white horses, representing the *quadriga Iovis* (Jove in a four-horse chariot). His face was stained red, the ivory sceptre surmounted by an eagle was in his hand, and he wore the triumphator's toga of purple and gold. Upon reaching the Capitol he dismounted and walked up, or, if he was feeling sufficiently superstitious, crept up, the steps to the shrine where he offered to the god his laurel crown. Frequently too he offered the *fasces,* the insignia of his rank, or a palm branch. Then followed a sacrifice and afterward a banquet in the temple, in which the senate and the officials of the state partook with the triumphator." See the end of II, 5 where Tibullus mentions the future triumph of Messalla's son Messalinus.

Syria was such a general term to classical writers that an adjective had to be used to identify the exact locality, in this case Palestine. The white dove was sacred to Astarte (Hebrew: Ashtoreth; Babylonian-Assyrian: Ishtar; Greek: Aphrodite), who was a Phoenician goddess of fertility and reproduction.

In the ancient world Tyre was something like Manhattan Island, too small for its enormous ocean commerce, especially in dyes, and for the crowding population its wealth invited. It grew upward in tiers of high buildings and palaces on the coast of Phoenicia. Aside from inventing the alphabet, the Phoenicians were the great early navigators.

The flooding of the Nile in summer, from mid-June to October, when rivers are usually low or dry, was a mystery and the more so because Egypt has no rainfall. The discovery of the source in the Nineteenth Century explained the mystery.

"Rain-bringing Jove" (*pluvio Iovi*) is probably the only Tibullian phrase which has come down into modern speech, as "Jupiter Pluvius." KFS notes that there are only five examples in all Latin writings, and they appear to be echoes of Tibullus. He feels, however, that the phrase hardly caught on in popular speech until after Goethe used it twice in poems and most likely transmitted it to us.

Ivy was sacred to Bacchus, who is here indistinguishable from Osiris. Saffron, or yellow, was a color particularly associated with him, though it was a sacred color in general. The bone flute (*tibia*) was another attribute of Bacchus and festal occasions.

The wicker box contained ceremonial objects.

Honey from Mount Hymettus in Attica was famous.

The memorial highway was commissioned by Augustus of the generals who were given triumphs. Each general was to repair certain sections of roadway and pay the expense from his war spoils. Messalla's assignment was a portion of the Via Latina which passed between Tusculum and the limestone Alban Hills southward to join the Via Appia at Beneventum.

Vitruvius, the engineer contemporary with Messalla, explained the method of making a Roman road. After the earth was graded and packed solid, a layer of rocks, with or without cement, was spread on it, and a layer of rubble mixed with lime was put on this and rammed to a nine-inch thickness; then a layer of paving stones was carefully fitted together on a bed of hard cement.

I,8

The second of the three elegies concerning the boy Marathus.

Tibullus covers the three principal methods of divination: fortune-telling, birds and sacrificial entrails. The fourth method, interpretation of the Sybilline Books, provides a motive in II, 5.

Knots were commonplaces of sorcery. One of the contemporary relics is the "true lover's knot."

Marathus, the *puer delicatus,* overdresses in feminine style and assiduously curls his hair, worn long since he is under age. This habit is acceptable enough for his status with the poet but hardly congruent with his new position as masculine lover of a girl.

The catalogue of spells and magical marvels is common in such references (I, 2). The belief that crops could be moved from one field to another by witchcraft was a persistent one; it appeared in witch trials from the Fifteenth to the Eighteenth Centuries. Eclipses were popularly believed to have been caused by witches drawing down the moon. Brass and bronze always have magic qualities, and the beating of metal gongs, drums or bells to frighten away demons or evil powers is widespread. In the case of eclipses, the objective was probably at first to frighten away a monster that was devouring the sun or moon.

Marathus's attractions as a *puer delicatus* would be destroyed by the emergence of a rough beard.

When Tibullus was writing, dyed blonde hair was especially stylish with women like Pholoë, who has captured Marathus from him. One of the dyes which might give hair this tint was taken from the juice of green walnut hulls.

"What's the glory" of an easy conquest (see note I, 6 on Cupid).

I,9

The last of the three elegies concerned with Marathus.

Tibullus knows quite well that lovers' vows can always be broken (I, 4). All the same, the perjurer of love invites the wrath of fierce Venus, and the goddess of vengeance always catches a sinner, sneaking up like Death, silently and often when least expected.

One or more linkboys bore torches or lanterns to light the way for those who ventured out at night, from ancient Greek and Roman days up to medieval times. Here Tibullus plays the slavish linkboy to Marathus on his visits to a girl.

Lucifer, though usually conceived as having wings, may have been given a rather unnecessary chariot by the Greeks. Most planetary deities had steeds and chariots (compare Sun and Moon). However, on the basis of remaining evidence in antique art, only Roman poets attributed a chariot to Lucifer, and KFS says it appears for the first time in this instance.

A palm wreath or branch was a symbol of victory, and thus it gives an air of "sour grapes" to the end of the elegy.

Epitaphs and votive inscriptions, so many of which are collected in the *Greek Anthology,* were regular motives of elegy.

I,10

On the "terrible sword" and war as the origin of man's woes, see I, 1; I, 2; I, 3.

The military campaign Tibullus refers to in this elegy could be either the mission with Messalla culminating in the victory at Actium (I, 3) or the expedition into Aquitania (I, 7).

The "wicker basket" contained the sacred objects used in the ceremony (I, 7).

Here is the usual opposition of happiness and the simple life (I, 5) to the evils of the Age of Iron: navigation, greed and luxury, and war (I, 1; I, 2; I, 3; II, 3).

The ferryman over the river Styx was Charon.

Romans held the still rather widespread belief that the dead retained in their ghostly appearances any wounds or traces of the cause of their death. In this case, Tibullus refers to the effects of the funeral pyres on the bodies.

The "lake of darkness" (*obscuros lacus*) is the rendering in Shakespeare's *King Lear,* Act III, Scene 6: "Nero is an angler in the lake of darkness."

II,1

Concerning a rural festival, but which one is uncertain. Some hold for the Ambarvalia, celebrated in early May, others for the Feriae Sementivae or Paganalia, in late January. The Ambarvalia ("going around the fields") was observed when blight and bad weather were most likely to ruin the just ripening crops. The ceremony consisted of a procession of the sacrificial victims, followed by olive-crowned worshipers, thrice around the boundaries of the field to be purified. After this, the sacrifice at the altar, the regular prayer and the customary rejoicing. This was the private ritual of individuals, and there was a broader ceremony to purify the Roman state, which KFS says still survives in Italy in the Litania Maior of Rogation Week.

Silence was customarily invoked in such rites to avoid any chance of utterance of ill-omened words. The poet, as head of the house, conducts the ceremony.

Gods usually bear and receive as offerings something suggestive of their attributes, thus grapes for Bacchus and grain for Ceres. The horns of Bacchus obviously symbolize virility and fertility.

Labor ceased on Roman holy days, just as it does on Christian and Jewish. Even those beasts that worked for man, here the oxen sacred to Ceres, had a holiday and festal decorations.

Purity, both sexual and physical, in religious rites continues to be important to this day.

"Gods of our fathers"—Tibullus avoids addressing specific gods and thus keeps the elegy typical of rustic celebrations. Cato, in "On Agriculture," gives the actual prayer for such an occasion.

Falernian wine was more heady than the mild Chian. It was smoky because the jars of immature wine were set on the hearth to age, and the jars were smoke-streaked. Today we might think of the taste of Scotch whisky.

The rise from barbarism to civilization, a favorite poetic theme, is here attributed to the country gods. Osiris gets the glory in I, 7; Saturn and his Golden Age in I, 3. Oak mast (acorns) was the traditional primitive food of man (II, 3).

The use of red cinnabar or paints was ceremonial. See I, 1 on Priapus and the notes to I, 7 on the triumphator.

The domestic gods (Lares) would guard the slave boys of a household as well as the owners.

The ancient loom stood upright, and the warp, attached to clay sinkers, hung down and rattled with each shuttling through and beating of the woof.

The invitation of Cupid to the scene of rustic festivity introduces the erotic subject conventional in elegy.

Ancient belief held that a prayer must be spoken, like a charm, in order to be heard by the gods; but no one would want to call aloud on Cupid and be overheard by friends except when praying for his herd.

The Phrygian tibia, frequent in orgiastic worship of Ops of Ida, was a straight tube of wood with a curving piece of metal or horn at the end.

KFS says that the closing picture of Night in her chariot, followed by her children, the stars, and by Sleep with great wings and then by Night's other children, Dreams, forms a unique one in classical literature, though most of the details had been suggested or described separately in earlier writings.

II,2

A birthday poem for Tibullus's friend Cornutus, who is possibly Cerinthus of the Sulpicia poems in "No Harm to Lovers."

Tibullus pretends to officiate as the priest in the ceremony for the Birth Spirit or Genius. Sacrifices to this Birth Spirit were always bloodless, since life must not be taken on the day life was given.

The Arabs and other Orientals were generally considered effeminate by Roman writers.

The "Eastern Sea" was red from the rising sun and was probably the Arabian Sea. The Red Sea (*Mare Rubrum*) of the ancients was not the present Red Sea but the Persian Gulf, an arm of the Arabian Sea. It was a common belief that its shores were littered with gems and pearls cast up by the tides.

II,3

The first of the four elegies concerned with Tibullus's affair with the girl Nemesis. There is a certain fitness in the poet's choice of this pseudonym for the girl; Nemesis is also the name of the goddess of justice and retribution, who punishes pride and arrogance. The address to his friend Cornutus, as that to Macer in II, 6, is merely a conventional pretext to begin his tale of woe.

KFS: ". . . Tibullus's object in choosing the girl was to 'get even' with Delia, and in christening her Nemesis he meant to indicate that in his case she was the mortal instrument of the great goddess of balance and of even-handed justice. If so, he found—as many others have found—that his instrument of vengeance was something of a boomerang." This Nemesis is arrogantly a courtesan, unlike Delia, and interested in nothing but the money and presents she can get.

Venus and Cupid move to the country because, as deities of love, they wish to follow their favorite votary.

The concept of the conventional ideal lover in elegy required the "slender limbs" and "tender hands" as well as the frailty and pallidness of I, 8 and the willingness to suffer pain and hardship for the beloved of I, 2 and III, 9.

Apollo's sister was Diana. As patroness of virgins, she was most proper indeed. His stepmother was Juno, patroness of marriage, and therefore not disposed to look with favor on the children of Jove's irregular unions. Of course no man or god, as KFS notes, could carry a calf and keep any shred of dignity; he also notes that the failure of the god of song to interest his own bovine audience is a unique touch.

Several favorite themes of elegy are interwoven here: the lost Golden Age *vs.* the present Iron Age, the greed which is fed by wars, the unavoidable decrees of Fate, the unknown rival who seems to be a rich parvenu whose wealth derived from military booty.

Samian and Cumaean dishes were not costly but were handsome, being usually red with decorations. Unless very conservative, the well-to-do would probably choose silver dishes.

"Swarthy attendants" from India were favorite house servants among the demimonde because they suggested the favors of foreign potentates. Similarly "blackamoors" in oriental garb were common in Seventeenth and Eighteenth Century England and France. The assumption that the tropics were hot because the sun was closer than in other regions and by its closeness darkened the skins of the people was common in ancient times.

The scarlet dye from Africa was made in Carthage from the berries of the scarlet oak. The purple dye of Tyre was made from the murex, a marine gastropod whose shell was used by Triton as a trumpet. Its color was genuine purple (deep violet) rather than the redder, cardinal purple of the Roman Church.

Barbarian slaves had their feet whitened with chalk or gypsum. All slaves, when put on the block for sale, were completely naked. The fact that Tibullus's rival, now rich through war plunder, had been offered for sale so often suggested to readers that even as a slave he was inferior.

II,4

The second of the four elegies dealing with Nemesis.

The path of the Sun, the Moon, etc., were treated in didactic poems such as Lucretius and Manilius wrote. Epics, like Homer's, were not for Tibullus either. Elegy was written, presumably, to win the favor of a mistress, but Nemesis has no taste for poems, only for cash.

The dead could not rest peacefully unless given the proper tributes, which might be repeated annually and on other specified occasions.

Since the household gods were the most intimate of guardian spirits, they would never be sold except from extreme poverty or extravagance.

Belief in the efficacy of "hippomanes" (horse-heat or horse-rage) mixed with herbs, as a love charm, was very old. Hippomanes meant not only the humour which flowed from cattle in heat, but the caul (part of the amnion) found often on the head of the newborn calf or foal.

II,5

Tibullus's longest poem, celebrating the installation of Messalla's eldest son, Messalinus, as one of the college of fifteen priests (*XV viri sacris faciundis*) in charge of the Sibylline Books. The date is uncertain, but since Messalinus's name appears for the first time at the end of the 17 B.C. list of the Quindecemviri, it was probably written not long before Tibullus's death in 19 B.C.

Phoebus Apollo was one of the first Grecian gods to be adopted by the Romans and became almost a national guardian. In 28 B.C. Augustus had built a great temple on the Palatine in gratitude for the triumph at Actium and set up in it the statue of Apollo Kitharoidos ("lyre-playing Apollo") by Skopas; this is the figure of the god which the poet describes. Invoked first as god of poetry and song, with an analogy between the victory at Actium and Jove's victory over Saturn (I, 3) for which Apollo wears the laurel crown of triumph, he is given, by implication, some credit for winning the battle in which Messalla fought. He is then invoked as god of prophecy. The "mantle expressly reserved" is the *palla,* an expensive costume which singers wore; it regularly appeared on Bacchus and Apollo in the aspect of *kitharoidos.*

Divination by interpretation of the books of the Sibyls is the important power bestowed by the god of prophecy in this poem. The other three prophecies mentioned here occur also in I, 3; I, 8; II, 1.

The "holy books"—the Sibylline Books—were a collection of oracles supposedly inspired in the Sibyls by Apollo. They had first been brought to Rome by Tarquin in the Fifth Century B.C. They were written in Greek hexameters, and the method by which particular ones were selected as applicable is not known. The selection was made by the Quindecemviri, which Messalinus was joining; they alone had the right of examining the books and then only by a special decree of the senate. From their scrutiny, they returned a written report, for the purpose not of foretelling events, but of discovering divine authority for action, usually in the case of prodigies such as those attending the murder of Julius Caesar described in the second parenthesis of this elegy. Several times the Sibylline Books were examined and deletions made in them, presumably to exclude fraudulent oracles, and they continued in existence in the temple on the Palatine as late as the Fifth Century A.D.

The Cumaean Sibyl had foretold that after the fall of Troy, Aeneas would found Rome.

KFS says this is the first instance of the application of the epithet, "eternal city," to Rome.

To avoid the swampy lowlands, early Romans built their primitive reed huts on the hillsides.

The passage in quotation marks is the direct prophecy of the Sibyl mentioned before the parenthetical diversion on Romulus.

Victory, the goddess, was usually represented with wings, and during battles she vacillated from one side to the other until her decision was made; then she hovered above the side she favored.

KFS says this is apparently the earliest reference in Roman literature to the "seven hills" of Rome.

The goddess of dawn, Aurora, opened the gates of morning so the chariot of the Sun, drawn by many horses, might ride up from the ocean. Oceanus, the Ocean Stream, was thought to girdle the earth, and its waters were life-giving and purifying (as was believed true of most moving water). The Sun and his team, after passing into darkness through the Gates of the Sun, entered a golden cup which Vulcan had forged for him and floated on Oceanus through the night back to the east.

The "new self" of Troy was, in the Aeneas legend, Troy reborn as Rome.

Laurel (bay, or sweet laurel), sacred to Apollo, is very mildly narcotic, but enough so for the ancients to believe it could induce oracular frenzy. The idea of peril in chewing it probably originated in the supposition that Apollo's spirit resided in the tree itself.

Virginity was a necessary condition for a prophetess; and flying hair was to be expected, since loose hair was customary in all rites and ceremonies, and the seeress must reach her inspired trance with much tossing of her head and gyrating.

The comet, torrent of stones, etc., were the portents and prodigies foretold by the Sibyls and relating to the assassination of Julius Caesar and the ensuing civil wars. Comets were widely believed to warn of general disaster for the people. The rain of stones, the noise in the sky and the clouding of the sun were probably caused by a very violent eruption of Mt. Etna which occurred not long before Caesar's murder. Weeping statues and speaking animals were (and still are) popular prodigies.

In burning, laurel crackles quite briskly, but the "good omen" was probably to be found in the extent to which it was burned—whether the fire went out leaving parts unconsumed, or whether it all burned to ashes.

The feast day to Pales was the Parilia (or Palilia), celebrated on April 21, and may be compared with the festival in II, 1. Leaping across the flames three times was part of the ritual—lustration by fire—and in itself was very widespread in Europe and the Orient and has survived into modern times.

The "jug kiss"—holding the ears like handles and drinking from the lips—was an ancient ceremonial in Tibullus's day and survived into this century in Italy as the "Florentine kiss."

War spoils and floats of conquered towns were paraded in the procession of a triumph (I, 7).

Wild bay was worn by the common soldiers as a protective against the vengeful spirits of warriors they had slain.

II,6

In this last elegy dealing with his girl Nemesis, Tibullus addresses his friend Macer only as a means of introducing Cupid and the theme of love. It is probable that Macer was Aemilius Macer, a poet of Verona, who died in Asia in 16 B.C. None of his didactic work survives. The date and the shortness of Book II, indicating posthumous publication, lead to the assumption that this elegy was Tibullus's last poem.

Slaves, here the love-slave, and the weak and helpless usually sought aid and sanctuary from higher powers (gods) or the dead, whose returning spirit could avenge the wrongs of the supplicant, now become protégé. The usual sign of displeasure among the dead was to send bad dreams to the malefactor. Ghosts look just as the human form did at the time of death (I, 10).

The procuress was customarily blamed for the infidelities, greed and coldness of the beloved and was subjected to verbal abuse.

III,19 and 20

There is some disagreement as to whether these poems are actually by Tibullus, are perhaps his juvenile work, or only by a member of Messalla's circle. J. P. Postgate argues that Tibullus did not write them; KFS takes the position that he very likely did.

NO HARM TO LOVERS
III,8

The Matronalia, observed on March 1, was the day on which slaves were feasted by their mistresses, somewhat as a counterpart of the Saturnalia, when they were feasted by their masters. Women put on their finest clothes and made sacrifices to their goddess, Juno, on the Esquiline. They always expected presents from any possible male—husband, lover or friend—and this poem probably accompanied such a gift from Tibullus to Sulpicia, the ward and niece of Messalla.

Mars is invoked because March is his month, and the first day was the Kalends, or his festival, as well as that of the women.

When indoors, women bothered little with their coiffure and wore simple white clothes (I, 3). For outdoors, their hair was elaborately dressed and their robes bright in color.

Vertumnus, as god of changing seasons, obviously had many costumes.

The first lyre was made by the infant Mercury from a tortoise shell, but he gave it to Apollo as a peace-offering for having stolen his sacred cattle.

Sulpicia is "worthy of the band" of Apollo and the Muses because of her ability to write the poems which follow this.

III,14

Messalla is unaware of Sulpicia's interest in Cerinthus and has not invited him on the journey.

Arretium (present Arrezzo) is near the source of the Arno, which is not really so "frigid" as Sulpicia subjectively considers it.

III,15

Cerinthus, as a young man of respectable class, may come to Messalla's house on a festal occasion such as a birthday.

III,12

Birthday Juno (*Iuno Natalis*) was the female counterpart of a man's Genius or Guardian Spirit.

Like Messalla, Sulpicia's mother does not realize where the girl's affections lie. It was fairly usual for a mother to suggest the prayers to be made.

On spoken and silent prayers, see II, 1; III, 11.

III,17

The fever is apparently malarial.

III,10

Disease was looked upon as a possession by demons and these had to be driven out by magic charms.

The gods will do "no harm to lovers," who, along with poets, madmen and drunks, are given their especial protection.

III,16

The toga suggests a woman of the lowest class of the demimonde, a hired girl who wasn't good enough to support herself by prostitution alone, but had to take in spinning to help out. On class distinctions in dress, and on spinning for hire by aged courtesans, see I, 6.

Servius (Sulpicius), says KFS, was "doubtless the son of Cicero's old friend." He had been dead a long time, which would explain Messalla's guardianship of Sulpicia.

III,9

Hunting wild boars was a favorite theme of erotic elegy; the best known examples concern Venus and Adonis. Tibullus, possibly posing again as Sulpicia while he writes, is obviously thinking of that pair of lovers. The boar was thought by the Romans to be the most dangerous of the animals they hunted in a sport which was distinctly for gentlemen only.

Cupid, as agent of Venus, is opposed to the "Delian Lady" or Diana of Delos, goddess of the hunt.

Nets were used to surround the quarry and were usually carried by a servant. Sulpicia, as all lovers are accustomed to do, will perform the work of a love-slave.

GLOSSARY

This glossary refers only to the English text. Easily identified geographical names which have been retained to the present day and personifications are not included unless some comment especially relevant to a poem can be made.

ADMETUS. (II, 3) A king in Thessaly, husband of Alcestis, whose herds were tended by Apollo. In the oldest account, the god was commanded by Zeus to serve Admetus for one year in punishment for having murdered, some say the Cyclops, some say their sons, and some say the Python. Tibullus's version, interpreting the servitude as caused by love, is Alexandrian and was a popular illustration of the power of love. In any event, Apollo secured from the Fates exemption from death for Admetus if someone else would die in his stead. His wife, Alcestis, chose to do so.

AENEAS. (II, 5) The Trojan hero of Vergil's *Aeneid* and one of the figures in the *Iliad*. His father was Anchises, his mother Venus. Through Venus, by a union with Mars or Cronus, he was half-brother of Cupid. Fleeing from burning Troy, he carried his father on his back with the household gods, wandered in ships for seven years, and finally reached Latium, where he married the king's daughter Lavinia and founded Rome. He shared honor for the latter deed with his descendant, Romulus (*q.v.*).

ALBA LONGA. (II, 5) A town on Lago Albano, founded thirty years after Aeneas's death by his son, Ascanius, whose mother is generally considered to have been Aeneas's first wife Creusa, daughter of Priam, king of Troy. She was lost in the sack of the city. Alba Longa is not a Latin name, but probably Ligurian for "mountain town"; the site is uncertain, but it may be at Castel Gandolfo.

AMALTHEA. (II, 5) The Sibyl of Cumae.

ANIO. (II, 5) A tributary of the Tiber River; it plunges in a cataract over rocks at Tibur (Tivoli).

APIS. (I, 7) See *Osiris*.

APOLLO. God of poetry, music, divination (II, 5), archery, healing (II, 3; III, 10); son of Jove and Latona (Greek Zeus and Leto). As Phoebus ("radiant one") he is poetically addressed by certain attributes of a sun-god. His twin sister was Diana, goddess of the hunt. They were born on the island of Delos, where both had shrines, though Apollo's chief oracle was at Delphi. As god of music and poetry, he presided over the nine Muses (II, 4; III, 8). Along with Bacchus, Apollo could never grow old; and, since the hair of Roman boys was never cut short until their majority, both these deities had long unshorn hair (I, 4; II, 3; II, 5; III, 10).

AQUITANIA. (I, 7; II, 1) A province in Gaul, situated between the Garonne, the Pyrenees and the Bay of Biscay.

ARRETIUM. (III, 14) A town in Etruria, now called Arezzo.

ASCANIUS. (II, 5) Son of Aeneas (*q.v.*), founder of Rome, and Creusa, daughter of Priam, king of Troy. About thirty years after his father's death, he founded Alba Longa.

ATTIC HONEY. (I, 7) The honey from the Hymettus mountains in Greece was famous. Tibullus uses an adjective based on the name of an ancient king of Attica (Greece), Mopsopus.

AUDE. (I, 7) A river in the ancient land of Aquitania (*q.v.*).

AURORA. (I, 3) Goddess of the dawn (II, 5); her father was either Hyperion (a Titan, the Sun or its father) or Pallas, a Titan; her mother was Terra, goddess of earth. By Tithonus, brother of King Priam of Troy, she bore Memnon who was killed by Achilles, and her tears of grief are seen as dewdrops. Another son, Lucifer ("light-bringing"), by Cephalus, was the morning star.

BACCHUS. God of wine, identical with Greek Dionysus, son of Zeus and Semele, daughter of Cadmus. The Greeks also identified him with Egyptian Osiris (I, 7) and the Romans with their ancient wine-god Liber. He was widely considered the promoter of grape culture. Like Apollo (*q.v.*) he was eternally youthful and his hair was never cut short (I, 4).

BELLONA. (I, 6) Goddess of war and sister of Mars. She had become merged by the first century with the Greek Enyo (war-goddess) and a Cappadocian goddess, Ma, whose rituals resembled those of Isis (I, 3) and the Great Mother, Cybele, or Ops of Ida (I, 4). Tibullus refers particularly to the Cappadocian goddess.

BIRTH SPIRIT. See *Guardian Spirit.*

BOY-GOD. See *Cupid.*

CAMPANIA. (I, 9) A level province in central Italy whose fields have always been proverbially fertile.

CERBERUS. (I, 3; I, 10) The watch-dog of Hades, the underworld. He had three heads, from which a mane of serpents grew or which bands of serpents circled at his necks, and a serpent's tail, which was sometimes conceived as ending in a snake's head. Thus, he was more dragon than dog, but, probably by association with watch-dogs at the door, he took on canine characteristics in the ancient mind.

CERES. Goddess of grain and the harvest, daughter of Saturn and Ops. She was goddess of plenty, identical with Terra (Earth).

CHARTRES. (I, 7) Ancient Autricum, situated on the Loire (Liger), chief town of the Carnutes, a people of Gaul.

CHIAN. (II, 1) Wine from the Isle of Chios (Scio) in the Aegean Sea. It was milder than Falernian wine, native of Italy.

CILICIA. (I, 2; I, 7) A province in southern Asia Minor.

CIRCE. (II, 4) An enchantress and sea-nymph, daughter of Helios (the Sun) and Perse (daughter of Oceanus). She was celebrated for her magic arts. She lived first at Colchis, an Asian province, where her brother Aeëtes was king, then on the island of Aeaea, near Latium. Her niece, daughter of Aeëtes, was Medea.

COAN, COS. (II, 3; II, 4) An island off the coast of Asia Minor. A type of silk similar to chiffon was manufactured there. Very expensive, it was popular especially among the demimonde. The Romans had no general name for silk and termed it according to the three varieties: *Coa* (from Cos), *bombycina* (from the Latin for silkworm) and *serica* (from the Latin for "people of Eastern Asia," i.e., the Chinese).

CORCYRA. (I, 3) An island in the Ionian Sea, today Corfu.

CORNUTUS. See Introduction.

CUMAE, CUMAEAN. (II, 3) From Cumae, a colony in Campania which made popular pottery. Cumae was also famous as the home of the Sibyl Amalthea (II, 5).

CUPID. The irresponsible god of love, son of Venus and Mars (or Mercury or Jove). His weapons against mortals were arrows or a flaming torch.

CYDNUS. (I, 7) A river in Cilicia, flowing through Tarsus.

CYTHEREAN. (III, 13) Venus; so called for the island of Cythera, where she rose from the sea foam and where stood the seat of her worship.

DANAUS. (I, 3) King of Argos, whose fifty daughters (the Danaïdes) were married to the fifty sons of his twin brother, Aegyptus. He forced them to murder their husbands on the wedding night. But two escaped the punishment in Hades meted out to the others for this crime against Venus: Hypermnestra, who spared her husband, and Amyone, who atoned by supplying water to drought-stricken Argos.

DAWN. See *Aurora*.

DELIAN LADY. (III, 9) Diana (*q.v.*).

DELOS. (II, 3) One of the Cyclades (islands in the Aegean), birthplace of Diana and her twin Apollo. Thus, it was one of the principal shrines of Phoebus Apollo.

DELPHI, DELPHIC. (II, 3) A city in Phocis, famous as the site of Apollo's chief oracle and shrine. It was formerly called Pytho.

DIANA. (I, 4; II, 3; II, 5; III, 9) The virgin goddess of the hunt and of the moon (mingling her attributes with those of Hecate, *q.v.*) and protectress of females. The twin sister of Phoebus Apollo, she was born of Jupiter and Latona, daughter of the Titan, Caeus, and Phoebe.

DOG DAYS, DOG STAR. (I, 1; I, 4; I, 7) The star Sirius in the constellation *Canis Major* and the brightest in the heavens. Its heliacal rising coincides with the sultriest part of summer, whence, "dog days."

ELIS. (I, 4) The most western province in the Peloponnesus and the site of the ancient Olympic games.

ELYSIAN FIELDS. (I, 3) The counterpart of the Golden Age in the afterlife, the Elysian Fields were located at the end of the world, usually beyond the Ocean Stream where the Sun rises and sets (II, 5), and usually beyond the gates of death.

EURUS. (I, 4; I, 5) The southeast wind, usually stormy and wild.

FALERNIAN, FALERNUM. (I, 9; II, 1) A region in Campania famous for its wines.

FATES. (I, 7; III, 11) Nona, Decuma and Morta, collectively called "Parcae" by the Romans, are best known by their Greek names: Clotho, who spins out the thread of life; Lachesis, who measures it; and Atropos, who cuts it off. At the hour of a man's birth, the web of his life was woven and all its events predestined. The Fates often sang prophetically at that time.

FORTUNE. (I, 5) The goddess of chance, or fate, who in Tibullus's poems plays a part, especially with her "wheel," similar to that of Nemesis, Vengeance, etc. The Wheel of Fortune seems to have appeared about the Third Century B.C. and had been preceded by the Ball of Fortune.

GARONNE. (I, 7) A river in Gaul, emptying into the Atlantic at the Bay of Biscay; the Santonians lived near its mouth.

GOOD GODDESS. (I, 6) *Bona Dea.* Her mysteries, along with the worship of Isis (I, 3), were considered by elegiac poets and many men as feminine pretexts to hide intrigues. The goddess seems to have been a combination of the ancient Italian goddess, Fauna (counterpart of Faunus, mythical king of Latium and grandson of Saturn) and Damia, a goddess of Magna Graecia. Fauna protected farmers, shepherds and agriculture; Faunus, under the name of Inuus, was god of fertility and later became confused with Pan. Worship of Damia was brought to Rome soon after 272 B.C., and men were rigidly excluded from the rites. The traditional punishment for any man who profaned the Good Goddess by looking on her or witnessing her rites was blindness, a punishment often meted out to others, even for secular breaches, as late as the Eleventh Century when "peeping Tom" spied on Lady Godiva in Coventry.

GUARDIAN SPIRIT. (I, 7) The *"Genius"* which guarded each person from birth to death and was especially worshiped on birthdays. Also referred to as "Birth Spirit" (II, 2), "Patron Spirit" (III, 11) and "Birthday Juno" (III, 12) where the sense is directed toward Juno as the Birth Spirit of women.

HADES. (II, 6) The abode of the dead, the underworld.

HECATE. (I, 1; I, 2; I, 5) The supreme goddess of magicians. She was the *Dea Triformis* (Triple Goddess, pictured with three heads or bodies), combining Luna (Selene) in heaven, Diana (Artemis) on earth, and Hecate in hell (Hades). Embodying two moon goddesses, she was ideal for charming the moon to descend to the earth. She haunted graves and crossroads and was worshiped at the latter (I, 1), where she was frequently called Trivia (I, 5) or, more familiar to us, "Diana of the Crossways." Her worship persisted into the Eleventh Century and the superstitions about crossroads into the contemporary era. Until recently, in some countries, suicides and vampires were buried at crossroads. The Witches' Sabbath no doubt derived from her cult. The baying of her hounds, still heard any night when there is a full moon and nearby dogs (for dogs can see things which we cannot), announces her approach.

HEROPHILE. (II, 5) A Sibyl, priestess of Apollo.

HOPE. (II, 6) The goddess, *Spes,* who had several temples in Rome.

IDA. (I, 4) Not the mountain in Crete usually indicated, but a high mountain in Phrygia, near Troy, where the worship of Cybele (called Ops [*q.v.*] by the Romans) originated.

ILIA. (II, 5) A vestal virgin, identical with Rhea Silvia, who was the mother of Romulus and Remus by Mars. The reference here is to the conception of those twins. The oldest versions of the story make Ilia a daughter of Aeneas, but because they ignore a time-gap of some 300 years, she is usually aligned with a vague branch of Alban kings descended from Aeneas and Lavinia and is given Numitor as father. She had gone to the sacred river Numicus to draw water. There a magic slumber fell upon her, and she was ravished by Mars, who generally descended from heaven in full armor. Livy suggests that Ilia may have been deceived in thinking her seducer was a god.

ISIS. (I, 3) Egyptian goddess, sister-wife of Osiris (*q.v.*), one of whose attributes was the power of healing sickness. Her worship had spread to Rome during the life of Sulla (138–78 B.C.) and continued to increase until the Third Century A.D. Many women of the lower classes were devotees of Isis, often for reasons of convenience, as with the Good Goddess (*q.v.*). In many ways—ideas, symbols, ascetic regulations and ritual, which included fasting, cleanliness (I, 1), periodic chastity (I, 6) and mortification—worship of Isis resembled Christianity and was for a long time a strong rival to it.

IXION. (I, 3) A king of the Lapithae in Thessaly. When Jupiter discovered that his wife Juno had been insulted and molested by Ixion in his passion, he hurled the audacious king into Tartarus (hell) where he was bound to a constantly revolving wheel. Some authors say the wheel was one of flames.

JOVE. The all-powerful ruler of heaven and earth, also called Jupiter, was the son of Rhea and Saturn (*q.v.*), who had reigned in the "Golden Age." Defeating and deposing his father, Jove ruled the universe, but to most poets it seemed an "Age of Iron" (I, 3; II, 3). He controlled the storms, lightning (I, 2) and rain (I, 7, as "Jupiter Pluvius") and was the chief patron of men. His sister and wife, Juno (*q.v.*), as goddess of women and marriage, disapproved of his many love affairs out of wedlock, and, when she caught him breaking his vows to her, he decreed that lovers' pledges need not be kept (I, 4).

JUNO. Goddess of the universe in the female division, as the sister-wife of Jove, she directs affairs of women, marriage, birth, etc. Because of her husband's irrepressible infidelity, she had become jealous, a protector of conventions and hostile to all the objects of Jove's attentions, whether other goddesses or mortals.

JUPITER. Contraction of *Iovis pater*. See *Jove*.

KALENDS. (III, 8) The first part of a month. See Notes to the Poems.

LARES. Tutelary gods of the household and its fields. In general, the Lar was an ancestral spirit which was propitiated with gifts and an undying flame on its shrine. The two principal divisions were the *Lares compitales*, those of fields and dwellings near the crossroads (I, 1), and the *Lares familiares*, strictly household deities which were set in a small shrine by the hearth or, in large houses, in a chapel near the entrance. The Lares apparently received more sacrifices than their associated divinities, the Penates (*q.v.*), being honored not only on monthly occasions and holidays, but on any occasion particularly touching the family: birthdays, marriages, departures on journeys or returns (I, 3), moving into a new house, reaching majority and death. The offerings consisted of incense, garlands, grape clusters and wine, though a favorite sacrificial offering among the Romans was a pig (I, 10). The spirits of the dead ancestors were represented by crude figures shaped from tree-trunks (compare the figure of Priapus, I, 4) and handed down through generations.

LATONA. (II, 3) Daughter of the Titan, Caeus, and Phoebe and the mother by Jove of Phoebus Apollo, who was the symbol of youth and manly beauty.

LAURENTIAN FIELDS. (II, 5) A region on the banks of the Tiber ruled by King Latinus, with whom Aeneas made a treaty when the Trojans landed in his country.

LAURENTUM. (II, 5) The first town founded by Aeneas in Latium, now known as Torre di Paterno.

LAVINIUM. (II, 5) The second town founded by Aeneas in Latium, and named for his wife, Lavinia, daughter of King Latinus.

LETHE, LETHEAN. (I, 3) A river in Hades. When its waters were drunk they caused forgetfulness of the past.

LOIRE. (I, 7) The longest river in modern France, emptying into the Bay of Biscay. Along part of it dwelt a tribe whose chief town is now called Chartres.

LOVE-GOD. See *Cupid.*

LUCIFER. (I, 3) The morning star; son of Aurora, goddess of the dawn, by Cephalus. Its appearance in the east heralds the dawn (I, 9).

LUCK. (I, 5) See *Fortune.*

MARPESSOS. (II, 5) A mountain in Paros.

MARS. The god of war and the lover of Venus (III, 8). Through his seduction of the vestal virgin, Ilia (*q.v.*), he became the father of Romulus, founder of the Roman nation (II, 5). He always came down from heaven in full armor.

MATRONALIA. (III, 8) See Notes to the Poems.

MEDEA. (I, 2; II, 4) Daughter of Aeëtes, King of Colchis, and, like her aunt Circe (*q.v.*), a famous sorceress. In the elegies at hand, she is not the towering figure of epic and tragedy, but the mistress of magical powers unknown to most men. In Tibullus's day, books which claimed to contain the charms and recipes of Medea and Circe were circulated.

MEMPHIS. (I, 7) An ancient city in middle Egypt, famous as the residence of the pharaohs. A great temple to Apis once stood there.

MINERVA. (I, 4; II, 1) Goddess of wisdom, war and arts, she sprang to life from Jove's brow. She was also the patroness of spinning (II, 1).

MUSES. The nine daughters of Jove and Mnemosyne (goddess of memory), who were divinities of song, poetry and the liberal arts (I, 9) and were presided over by Apollo (II, 4; III, 8). Pieria, in the region of Mt. Olympus, was their ancient haunt and principal place of worship, and they were therefore called Pierian maidens (I, 4; III, 8). The nine: Clio (history), Calliope (heroic poetry), Erato (love poetry), Euterpe (music and lyric poetry), Melpomene (tragedy), Polyhymnia (sacred songs), Terpsichore (dancing and choral song), Thalia (comedy and idyllic poetry) and Urania (astronomy).

NEMESIS. In Book II, not the goddess of retribution, but the name of Tibullus's girl.

NEREID. (I, 5) A sea-nymph or mermaid. Nymphs were of several sorts: Nereids, who were the 50 daughters of the sea-god Nereus and Doris, daughter of Oceanus, and lived in the sea; dryads and hamadryads, who lived in trees; naiads, who lived in lakes, rivers and springs; and oreads, who lived in mountains.

NISUS. (I, 4) A king of Megara who had a purple lock of hair which protected his realm. His daughter Scylla (not the one coupled with Charybdis) fell in love with Minos, king of Crete, who was besieging the city. She cut off the purple lock and betrayed the city to the enemy, only to have her beloved despise her and reject her advances.

NUMICUS. (II, 5) Once a large stream in Latium, thought to be possessed of magical powers. Its waters were used in the worship of Vesta, goddess of the hearth and its fire. In general, it had great religious importance for the whole of Latium and a native god (*deus indiges*) was worshiped there. Aeneas (*q.v.*) died near the stream, but the exact manner of his death is uncertain. Some think he was killed in battle and his body never discovered; others think he drowned in the Numicus. Venus besought her father Jove to allow her son to become a god; she ordered the Numicus to wash from Aeneas all that was mortal, and, thus deified, he was taken into heaven as Jupiter Indiges (Native Jupiter).

OCEAN. (I, 7) Oceanus, god of the Ocean Stream, which was thought to surround the disc of earth; or, to Romans, the Atlantic.

OLYMPUS. (I, 6; III, 8) A high mountain in Greece between Thessaly and Macedonia, thought to be the home of the gods.

OPS. (I, 4) Ops of Ida (*q.v.*) was Cybele, the Great Mother (associated with Greek Rhea, wife of Saturn), whose worship originated near Mount Ida in Phrygia and spread all over the Roman Empire. Her priests, self-castrated to emulate her beloved Attis (who is celebrated in spring ceremonies of resurrection here referred to), were called Galli, while other attendants were Corybants and Dactyli. All indulged in orgiastic rites, frenzied dance and song, self-mutilation and transvestism. From town to town they drew a shrine of the goddess wearing a turreted crown, and begged alms, sold charms, prophesies, etc. They were generally considered a scurrilous lot of homosexuals.

OSIRIS. (I, 7) Brother and husband of Isis (*q.v.*) and the Egyptian father of civilization, agriculture, viniculture and, in the latter function, a counterpart of Bacchus-Dionysus. In his revival after death, he is a deity of spring bringing the sun back to earth after the darkness of winter, his period of death. During death he was reincarnated on earth as Apis (*q.v.*), the sun god, represented as a bull, which in turn died and became Serapis, or the original Osiris. (The Nile, when spoken of as a divinity by Egyptians, was called H'api; Osiris had been cut to pieces and cast into the river.) There was a great temple to Apis at Memphis.

PALATINE. (II, 5) One of the famous seven hills of Rome. The others are the Capitoline ("Jove's Hill"), Aventine, Caelian, Esquiline, Quirinal and Viminal.

PALES. (I, 1; II, 5) "The one who feeds." A rustic tutelary deity of shepherds and cattle. She was an ancient goddess of Latium, and her statue, rough-hewn like those of Pan and Priapus, stood in the woods or open fields. Her celebration in the springtime Palilia, or Parilia (II, 5), was distinctively a shepherd's festival and, among other rites, involved the pouring of milk over the image of the goddess.

PALESTINIAN SYRIA. (I, 7) See Notes to the Poems.

PAN. (II, 5) Son of Mercury and Penelope; a rustic divinity of forests, pastures, flocks and shepherds. A regular offering to him was milk, as it was to Pales. The ilex, the beech and the pine were especially sacred to him, and his statue was often set beneath such a tree. He was given to sportive dancing and playing on the pipes, which he had invented, and which the shepherds adopted.

PATRON SPIRIT. (III, 11) See *Guardian Spirit.*

PEACE. (I, 10) Pax, the goddess of peace, was usually conceived as robed in white, holding an ear of corn and other general attributes of prosperity. Consider the modern expression coupling "peace and plenty."

PELEUS. (I, 5) King of the Myrmidons in Thessaly, who loved Thetis (*q.v.*).

PELOPS. (I, 4) The ancestor of the house of Atreus (Agamemnon and Menelaus). His father, Tantalus (*q.v.*), served him up as a dinner for the gods, but they quickly discovered the crime and reassembled all his parts except one shoulder already eaten by Ceres. Having replaced the shoulder with ivory, they restored Pelops to life.

PENATES. (I, 3) Guardian deities of the household, usually coupled with Lares (*q.v.*). By extension, including as they did the private and personal Lares, they became the spirit protectors of the state conceived as a family of citizens.

PHAROS, PHARIAN. (I, 3) The island in the harbor of Alexandria on which Ptolemy II built the famous lighthouse. It was probably the point from which the cult of Isis (*q.v.*) embarked for Rome.

PHOEBUS. See *Apollo.*

PHRYGIA, PHRYGIAN. (I, 4; II, 1) A country in Asia Minor whose people were noted for indolence. It was the seat of the orgiastic worship of Ops (*q.v.*).

PIERIAN MAIDENS. See *Muses.*

PRIAPUS. (I, 1; I, 4) God of male procreation and of gardens, orchards and vineyards; said to be the son of Aphrodite and Dionysus. His figure was usually rough-hewn from a tree-trunk, often painted red (I, 1), phalliform (hence his appropriateness for discoursing of love) and not handsome. He always carried a curved billhook, was set up outdoors in cultivated plantations, naturally took on the function of a scarecrow (I, 1) and an association with another bucolic god, Pan. Priapic worship continued for centuries after the founding of the Christian church and was violently attacked by the early Fathers.

PYRENEES. (I, 7) The mountain range dividing France and Spain, named for Pyrene, beloved of Hercules, who was buried there.

PYTHO. (II, 3) Ancient name for Delphi. By extension, the Sibyl of Delphi was called Pytho or the Pythoness.

REMUS. (II, 5) Twin brother of Romulus (*q.v.*).

RHONE. (I, 7) "The swift-flowing" (*Rhodanus*), a river in Gaul rising in the Alps and emptying in the Mediterranean Sea.

ROMULUS. (II, 5) Son of Mars and the vestal priestess, Ilia (*q.v.*). He and his twin brother Remus are famous in legend as the babes who were cast away by their outraged grandfather, King Numitor, and then suckled by a wolf. (Livy says the twins may have been brought up by a prostitute, known as a *lupa* [she-wolf].) Romulus shares with Aeneas (*q.v.*) the honor of being father of the Roman race. Aeneas came to Latium after the destruction of Troy, about 1184 B.C., married Lavinia, daughter of King Latinus, and founded the city of Lavinium. Some three hundred years later, Romulus and Remus were born to his descendant, Ilia. Romulus laid out the city of Rome and became its first king. Because Remus mockingly jumped over the city walls, Romulus killed him.

SAMIAN. (II, 3) A pottery ware made in Samos, an island in the Aegean Sea.

SANTONIANS. (I, 7) An Aquitanian tribe living near the mouth of the Garonne River.

SAÔNE. (I, 7) A river in Gaul, tributary of the Rhone.

SATURN. (I, 3; II, 5) Son of Uranus and Gaea. A Titan, he ruled over the Golden Age after overthrowing his father and was in turn overthrown by his son Jove (Greek Zeus). Saturn ("the Sower") was a god of agriculture and was celebrated in the Saturnalia in mid-December, an occasion for riotous fun, drinking, feasting, giving presents and lighting candles; it was absorbed by the Christian Fathers into our Christmas.

SIBYLS. (II, 5) Prophetesses. They had a variety of names, based on the location of the shrines where they prophesied; thus, it is possible they could all have been only one person who visited many places. They cannot be disentangled, but all were closely associated with worship of Apollo. Their prophecies were supposedly collected in the Sibylline Books.

SIBYL OF TIBUR. (II, 5) Albunea, who was later worshiped as a goddess. The famous temple of the Sibyl on the cliff below the falls of the Anio at Tivoli (Tibur) was probably hers.

STYX, STYGIAN. (I, 10) The river in Hades, the infernal regions, across which Charon ferried the dead from the world.

TANTALUS. (I, 3) A king of Phrygia, son of Jove, and father of Pelops (*q.v.*) and Niobe. Jove invited him to a banquet of the gods, but because he served his son's flesh to them (or stole their nectar, or revealed their secrets), Jove set him in Tartarus with water rising to his chin, only to recede when he tried to drink, and with fruit hanging over his head, only to withdraw when he reached. One of the favorite legends of the past as well as the present, it has given us the word "tantalize." A third punishment of an overhanging stone is also frequently mentioned, but Tibullus selects only the first.

TARBELLIANS. (I, 7) A tribe of Aquitanian Gauls living near modern Dax in the foothills of the Pyrenees.

TAURUS. (I, 7) A high mountain range in Cilicia in which the Cydnus rises.

THESSALY. (II, 4) A country in the northeastern part of Greece, and a fabled land of magic. Popular legend said that Medea (*q.v.*), when flying on a dragon away from Jason after killing their children and his new bride, emptied her box of magic herbs over the land.

THETIS. (I, 5) A nereid (*q.v.*) beloved of Peleus, king of the Myrmidons in Thessaly, by whom she bore Achilles. Tibullus follows Ovid's story: Peleus tried to ravish Thetis while she slept in her cave, to which she rode on a harnessed dolphin. But she had the magic ability to change shapes and foiled him until he was told by Proteus (equally changeable) how to conquer her.

TIBUR. (II, 5) Present-day Tivoli. See *Sibyl of Tibur.*

TISIPHONE. (I, 3) One of the three Furies. She was the archtorturer of Hades. Her associates were Alecto and Megaera.

TITIUS. (I, 4) See Notes to the Poems.

TITYOS. (I, 3) A giant who attacked Latona and was slain by her children, Apollo and Diana.

TRIVIA. (I, 5) Goddess of the crossroads, or Hecate (*q.v.*).

TROY, TROJAN. (II, 5) City of King Priam, destroyed by the Greeks (as told in the *Iliad*), from which Aeneas fled, eventually to found Rome, the "new" Troy.

TURNUS. (II, 5) King of the Rutuli. He had been promised Lavinia as his wife, but King Latinus, her father, heeding an oracle, gave her to Aeneas. Turnus then made war on Aeneas and set fire to his fleet, but Cybele transformed the ships into Naiads. In the conflict Turnus was killed.

TUSCULUM. (I, 7) Present-day Frascati.

TYRE, TYRIAN. A seaport in Phoenicia, famed for navigation and commerce and especially for its purple dyes, which were highly esteemed in the ancient world.

VELABRUM. (II, 5) A flat marshy area frequently overflowed by the Tiber and lying between the Capitoline, Palatine and Aventine hills in Rome.

VENGEANCE. (I, 8; I, 9) The goddess *Poena* who metes out inescapable punishment for wrong-doing, pride and arrogance. Similar in concept to Nemesis, goddess of retribution.

VENUS. Goddess of sensual love, who is very fierce toward anyone who disobeys her will.

VERTUMNUS. (III, 8) God of the changing seasons, who obviously had many costumes.

VESTAL FIRES. (II, 5) Vesta, daughter of Saturn and Ops, was goddess of the hearth and domestic life. In her temples the priestesses were obliged to be virgins and to keep the fire always burning on her altar.

VULCAN. (I, 9) Son of Jove and Juno and god of fire and the arts of the forge.

HUBERT CREEKMORE

1907–1966

One of America's leading Southern literary figures, Hubert Creekmore achieved wide recognition for his skill and authority in a broad range of literary endeavors.

Born in Water Valley, Mississippi, Mr. Creekmore graduated from the University of Mississippi, attended the Yale University School of Drama, and received his master's degree from Columbia University.

The author of three novels, *The Welcome, The Chain in the Heart,* and *The Fingers of Night* (reprinted as *Cotton Country*), and of three volumes of poetry, *Personal Sun, The Stone Ants,* and *The Long Reprieve,* Mr. Creekmore also edited collections of world poetry and medieval lyrics and translated the satires of Juvenal. He completed his translation of *The Book of True Love* by Juan Ruiz, Archpriest of Hita, just prior to his death.

His numerous book reviews and critical essays appeared in prominent newspapers and magazines, including *The New York Times Book Review, Poetry, The Nation,* and *Accent.*